Chapter 1
Would I Want Me for a Teacher?

> **Focus**
>
> 1. To analyze individual learning styles and educational philosophies.
> 2. To discuss how individual teacher needs impact classroom teaching and management.

Concerns of Beginning Teachers

As Mary, a first year middle school teacher, sat in her car at the end of the day, she swore that she would never return to State Middle School again in her life! Everything had gone wrong. She was exhausted from spending the last 4 days getting her classroom ready, and to make matters worse, she woke up late this morning and arrived at school 10 minutes before her students entered the classroom. No course at her university had really prepared her for this "real world" classroom experience. She was expected to know too much, to manage 30 students she had never met, and to maintain a super human energy level. On top of that, the assistant principal had the nerve to ask for lesson plans and a lunch count. Two mothers arrived at the classroom unannounced to inquire about a supply list, her neatly printed classroom roster was destroyed by changes, and students chattered uncontrollably. It was all too overwhelming. As she started her car's engine, she wondered how anyone could ever survive a career in teaching.

Experiences like Mary's first day, unfortunately, take their toll on many beginning teachers. Over and over, new teachers ask for more training in the areas of classroom management. In a recent survey of students completing their student teaching semester in all areas (Grades 1-12), the participants rated classroom management as the topic in which they needed and wanted more training. Other areas of concern were finding a job and working with special education students in the "regular" classroom. From the survey, these beginning teachers wrote:

> I feel that classroom management was an area I was most weak in. I feel that this could have been a much stronger aspect of my student teaching experience.

> The only suggestion that I have to offer after completing my first year as a teacher is to include more mandatory classroom management instruction and more exposure to the "real world" of teaching (extra paperwork, codes/ committees, PTA, discipline, etc.).

> There needs to be a classroom management class required for all education majors!

> Before student teaching, I felt very prepared, but when I entered the student teaching semester, I realized I needed more knowledge of discipline, management, and meeting individual differences.

> I had the most trouble with discipline during my student teaching semester.

Preparing beginning teachers for the modern classroom is not an easy task since there are so many variables to consider. One first year teacher compared her teacher education program to "boot camp" and her teaching experience to the real "war." She described daily occurrences as "battles" and daily assessed her performance based on whether or not she had "won or lost the battle." At the end of the year she reflected that she had "lost some battles," but by June, she had "won the war." Unfortunately, it is impossible to prepare new teachers for every "battle" that they might encounter; however, self-assessment and basic organizational strategies and management skills can better prepare them for a successful teaching career.

Classroom Management for Beginning Teachers

Third Edition

Shirley W. Jacob, Ph.D.

Southeastern Louisiana University
Hammond, Louisiana

The McGraw-Hill Companies, Inc.
Primis Custom Publishing

New York St. Louis San Francisco Auckland Bogotá
Caracas Lisbon London Madrid Mexico Milan Montreal
New Delhi Paris San Juan Singapore Sydney Tokyo Toronto

McGraw-Hill Higher Education

A Division of The McGraw-Hill Companies

Classroom Management for Beginning Teachers

17 18 19 20 QSR QSR 0 9 8 7

ISBN-13: 978-0-07-235710-3
ISBN-10: 0-07-235710-X

Editor: Judy Wetherington
Cover Design: Mark Anderson
Printer/Binder: Quebecor World

Table of Contents

To the Students

Welcome to teaching! This workbook is the product of ten years of listening to pre-service and beginning teachers express their concerns, frustrations, and inadequacies about teaching and their teacher preparation. They were tired of the theoretical "fluff" and wanted "bottom line" things to do. Therefore, each chapter of this working text is in response to a specific need and is designed to help you as a new teacher think about yourself, your students, and your classroom.

Chapter 1 is a self-assessment overview as you begin to know yourself, your personal needs, and the compromises you will eventually make in the classroom. Chapter 2 contains information about the job search as you look for a school district with a comparable philosophy. Included within that chapter are checklists to prepare and organize you for the first day of class. Chapter 3 allows you to reflect on the physical room itself and to develop a room arrangement to meet your teaching style. Establishing classroom routines is the focus of Chapter 5. Routines (procedures) are an important component of the overall management process since they "drive" your class forward through the school year. NOTHING takes the place of good classroom routines.

Beginning with Chapter 5, the "modern" student is described through his/her basic needs in school. The purpose of this chapter is to have you look with new eyes at a population of students who sometimes lack direction and a sense of responsibility. It attempts to help you understand how students use inappropriate behavior to satisfy their needs. Classroom rules, rewards, and consequences are the topics of Chapter 6. New teachers are given the opportunity to develop and to analyze classroom rules and make judgments concerning the use of rewards. Punishment and logical consequences are also contrasted. Chapter 7 introduces you to MLS students (Mean Little Sugars) and gives specific strategies to deal with their problem behaviors.

One thing that beginning teachers fear is a parent. Chapter 8 discusses the role of parents in their child's education and provides tips for conferencing with them. Finally, the workbook concludes with the development of your personal management plan. You will be asked to examine comprehensively the content of the workbook and write a plan that meets your needs.

Throughout the workbook are Quick Tip pages that provide a very brief synopsis of a concept or procedure. Also are example sheets to be used for personal accountability, rewards, and samples. At times, you will be asked to reflect on specific questions related to classroom management. Use these pages to express yourself openly since their purpose is to have you process information. Activities in each chapter are designed to help you develop your management plan and to check for understanding of a concept.

Finally, no one has the answer to the perfect classroom. There are many variables to consider as you begin your teaching career. This workbook is a small step to truly understanding yourself and your students. Good luck!

A special thanks to . . .

all of the classroom teachers who gave me advice while compiling this workbook, to my students who readily critiqued the contents, and to my family who shared me with my computer.

Self-Assessment

Why do teachers teach the way they do? From where do they get their classroom rules and procedures? Why is one teacher's classroom more noisy than another teacher's room? There is no one answer to any of these questions. Teachers generally teach and manage their classrooms in the ways that they were taught, in the ways that they learn best, in the ways that more information can be covered, and in the ways that best address personal needs and educational philosophies. Self-awareness is knowing who you are, what you believe in, and how you plan to achieve your goals in life. The next several pages are self awareness activities in which you will reflect on your choice of teaching as a career and then complete self-tests on learning styles and educational belief systems. It is important that you honestly respond to each item to better understand yourself and to project how your own preferences will impact your classroom management style. After the tests for learning styles and educational beliefs are self score sheets with explanations of the test categories.

Activity 1 -A
Career Choices

1. Is teaching your first career choice? If no, what is it?

2. How old were you when you realized that you wanted to become a teacher?

3. What are the main reasons you selected teaching as a career? Prioritize this list.

4. What are your career goals five years from now? Ten? Twenty?

   Five years:

   Ten years:

   Twenty years:

5. After your teaching career, how would you like to be remembered?

Activity 1-B
Learning Styles Indicator

Instructions: In the blank to the left of the number, write the letter that best describes your preference.

___ 1. I base my decisions on facts.
    a. most of the time
    b. some of the time
    c. seldom
    d. never

___ 2. I am careful and deliberate in planning.
    a. most of the time
    b. some of the time
    c. seldom
    d. never

___ 3. I approach problems logically.
    a. most of the time
    b. some of the time
    c. seldom
    d. never

___ 4. It is important that I understand how all of the pieces fit together to form the whole.
    a. most of the time
    b. some of the time
    c. seldom
    d. never

___ 5. I am led by my mind rather than my heart.
    a. most of the time
    b. some of the time
    c. seldom
    d. never

___ 6. I am more interested in the process rather than the product of an assignment.
    a. most of the time
    b. some of the time
    c. seldom
    d. never

___ 7. If I could choose between being an accountant and an dramatist, I would
       choose accounting.
       a. most of the time
       b. some of the time
       c. seldom
       d. never

___ 8. I like to make decisions based on facts and not feelings
       a. most of the time
       b. some of the time
       c. seldom
       d. never

___ 9. I prefer to study at a designated place
       a. most of the time
       b. some of the time
       c. seldom
       d. never

___10. If given a choice, I would rather analyze rather than synthesize
       a. most of the time
       b. some of the time
       c. seldom
       d. never

___11. I learn best by lecture.
       a. most of the time
       b. some of the time
       c. seldom
       d. never

___12. I am better at remembering names rather than faces.
       a. most of the time
       b. some of the time
       c. seldom
       d. never

___13. I am an early morning person.
       a. most of the time
       b. some of the time
       c. seldom
       d. never

___14. I prefer objective type test items rather than subjective items.
    a. most of the time
    b. some of the time
    c. seldom
    d. never

___15. I like time limits set on specific tasks.
    a. most of the time
    b. some of the time
    c. seldom
    d. never

___16. I like to have my work space neat and organized.
    a. most of the time
    b. some of the time
    c. seldom
    d. never

___17. I prefer the stability rather than change.
    a. most of the time
    b. some of the time
    c. seldom
    d. never

___18. I like to finish one project before I begin another.
    a. most of the time
    b. some of the time
    c. seldom
    d. never

___19. I prefer to study in a well-lit room.
    a. most of the time
    b. some of the time
    c. seldom
    d. never

___20. I prefer to work alone rather than in a group.
    a. most of the time
    b. some of the time
    c. seldom
    d. never

____21. **I read for facts and details rather than a general overview.**
      a. most of the time
      b. some of the time
      c. seldom
      d. never

____22. **I outline information in my notes.**
      a. most of the time
      b. some of the time
      c. seldom
      d. never

____23. **I break big assignments down into smaller sub-parts.**
      a. most of the time
      b. some of the time
      c. seldom
      d. never

____24. **I prefer assignements that are specific and well structured rather than open-ended.**
      a. most of the time
      b. some of the time
      c. seldom
      d. never

____25. **I prefer to be in a quiet place to study.**
      a. most of the time
      b. some of the time
      c. seldom
      d. never

Self Score: Use the following point system to score your test.

All "a" answers - 4 points
All "b" answers - 3 points
All "c" answers - 2 points
All "d" answers - 1 point

55 - 100 - Left Brain
46 - 54 - Whole Brain
0 - 45 - Right Brain

My score is: _____ ; According to this test, I am _____ .

****

What does this mean? Basically, as a learner, you have preferences for how, when, and what you learn. The following are some characteristics of left and right brain learners. Although you may not display all of the characteristics listed under each category, you will have a tendency to favor items under you learner heading and will have a tendency to teach based on your learner preference.

LEFT	RIGHT
Prefers verbal instruction	Prefers visual instruction
Remembers names	Remembers faces
Prefers not to eat or drink while learning	Prefers to eat and drink while learning
Prefers to complete a single task before starting another	Prefers to have several tasks to complete at one time
Prefers to work alone	Prefers to work with others
Prefers a formal environment	Prefers an informal environment
Prefers bright lights	Prefers dim lights
Prefers quiet	Prefers background noise
Prefers stuctured assignments	Prefers open-ended assignments
Prefers words to express meaning	Prefers body language to express meaning
Prefers to process information in sequence	Prefers to process information in patterns
Prefers to read for details	Prefers to read for an overview
Prefers intellectual activities	Prefers creative activities
Prefers to outline information	Prefers to summarize information
Prefers logical appeal	Prefers emotional appeal

Activity 1 - C
Educational Belief System Ranking Form

Directions: In the space provided, rank each of the following statements from 1(most important) to 5 (least important) according to your personal priorities and belief systems.

_____ 1. To develop students' abilities to think clearly, to use intellectual reasoning to solve problems, and to make rational decisions.

_____ 2. To nurture the individual child's unique potentials; to allow full development of his/her creativity and sensitivity, and to encourage personal integrity, love of learning, and self-fulfillment.

_____ 3. To diagnose the learner's needs and abilities, to design instructional strategies which develop skills and competencies, and to produce trained people who are able to function efficiently in our ever-changing complex technological society.

_____ 4. To transmit to young people the basic knowledge, skills, traditions, academic concepts, and values necessary to interpret, participate in, and further the heritage and traditions of our country.

_____ 5. To create a future world condition of peace, harmony, equality, and love; and to foster a new society with humans who can live together in balance with their environment and with each other.

Reprinted with permission
*Developed by the Institute for Intelligent Behavior, Berkeley, CA

Interpreting Your Beliefs

1. If you ranked statement one as your first choice, you could probably be classified as a cognitive processor, drawn to educational theorist and authors such as Jerome Bruner, Hilda Taba, Robert Sternberg, Jean Piaget, Reuven Feurstein, Maria Montessori, and Edward deBono. With your orientation to cognitive psychology, you may believe that the central role of schools is to develop rational thought processes, problem solving and decision making. You believe that the information explosion is occurring at such a rapid rate that is no longer possible for experts in any field to keep up with new knowledge. Thus we no longer know what to teach but instead must help students learn how to learn. You most like select instructional strategies that involve problem solving and the inquiry method. When you talk about instruction, you use terms from Bloom's Taxonomy, intellectual development, cognitive processes, metacognition, and thinking skills. You organize teaching around the resolution of problems using the Socratic Method and bring in discrepant events for students to explore and analyze. You evaluate students by how well they perform in problem solving situations. Your metaphorical model of education is that of information processing: Human beings are meaning makers and schools and teachers mediate those capacities.

2. If you marked the second item as most important, you could be termed a self-actualizer. With an orientation to Gestalt psychology, you regard schools as child-centered. You probably view the teacher as a facilitator for learning, and you believe the purpose of teaching is to bring out the unique qualities, potentials, and capacities in each child. You like multisensory instruction with many opportunities for auditory, visual, and kinesthetic learning. You value student choice whether it be for classroom topics, the nature of assignments, or classroom activities. You also

value self-directed learning and individualized instruction. To provide for students' multiple needs, interests, and developmental tasks, you use learning centers focused around themes. You value student autonomy and look for increases in autonomy as a central measure of your effectiveness as a teacher. You are drawn to such humanists as Abraham Maslow, Sylvia Ashton Warner, Arthur Combs, Carl Rogers, Sidney Simon, and George Leonard. Your vocabulary includes words referring to the affective domain and terms such as the whole child, nurturing, peak experiences, choice, democracy, holistic, self-esteem continuous progress, dignity, creativity, climate for learning, individualize, and caring. Because every child is different, you are concerned with developmentally appropriate curriculum, whole language, and creativity. Your metaphoric model of education is one of nurturing each child's potential.

3. If you ranked the third item on the survey as number one, it's likely that you have strong leanings toward the technologist position. You may be influenced by the behavioral psychology of Skinner, Pavlov, and Thorndike and may be attracted to such education authors as Robert Mager, James Popham, and Madeline Hunter. You place strong emphasis on accountability and measurable learning. Your metaphor for education is as an input--throughput--output system in which data and opportunities to learn skills are provided. You are skilled at task analysis and the instructional materials that might interest you are computers and learning systems with opportunities to diagnose entry levels and prescribe according to what is known and what is yet to be learned. You are probably more field independent and skilled in detail, with great ability to analyze, project, and plan. You talk about accountability, evaluation, task analysis, time-on-task, mastery, templates, diagnosis, prescriptions, disaggregated analysis, and percentiles.

4. If you ranked the fourth item as number one, you may regard yourself as an academic rationalist. Some of the philosophic company you keep includes Diane Ravitch, E.D. Hirsch, Arthur Bestor, William Bennett, and Chester Finn. You are drawn to teacher centered instruction believing that knowledgeable adults have the wisdom and the experience to know what is best for students. Your metaphor for education is the transmission of the major concepts, values, and truths of society, and you consider students as clay to be molded or as vessels to be filled. You value and are highly oriented toward increasing the amount and rigor of student learning. You are probably drawn to essential truths, the classics, and traditional values. You appreciate basic texts and the teaching strategies of lecture, memorization, demonstration, and drill. You evaluate students through summative examinations, achievement testing, and content mastery. You speak about discipline, authority, humanities, basics, scholarship, standardized tests, basic skills, and other aspects that value higher academic standards.

5. If you rated number five as your first choice, you probably are a social reconstructionist. You may be concerned with the problems of society, the shrinking world, the future of the planet, and major crises such as destruction of the food chain, the hole in the ozone layer, and the deforestation of timberland, protection of wildlike, and the threat of overpopulation. You view the learner as a social being--a member of a group, a responsible citizen, and one who identifies with and is proactive regarding the environmental ills and social injustices of the day. You probably agree with Nesbitt, who reports that we have gone beyond the age of representative democracies. Because we no longer trust our elective officials to make iimportant decisions, we have moved to a stage of participative democracies. You believe this is a world where we must care for our neighbors and take action as the grassroots level. As a teacher, you engage your students in recycling centers,

contributing to social issues, cooperative learning, outdoor education, and global education. Your metaphor of education is as an instrument of change, and you believe that schools are the only institution in our society charged with the responsibility of bringing about a better future and a better world. You are drawn to Marilyn Ferguson, Willis Harmon, Alvin Toffler, Robert Samples, John Naisbitt, and Jean Houston. Your vocabulary includes terms such as environment, consumer education, peace, student rights, multicultural, futurist, global intellect, pluralistic, change, save-the-Earth, ecology, and love.

REFLECTION

1. Based on the results of these tests, describe yourself in one sentence.

2. In one sentence, describe your classroom.

3. Honestly, how would you like to have you as a teacher? List 5 advantages and 5 disadvantages.

Advantages	Disadvantages
A.	
B.	
C.	
D.	
E.	

4. What can you do to address some of the disadvantages of having you as a teacher?

Chapter 2
Getting Started: The Countdown Begins

Focus
1. Write a resume.
2. Identify the importance of pre-planning to management.
3. List a sequence of activities to be completed before the first day of school.
4. Develop a list of general school supplies.

Finding a Job

PLEASE NOTE: APPLYING FOR A TEACHING POSITION VARIES FROM SCHOOL DISTRICT TO SCHOOL DISTRICT. BELOW ARE GENERAL GUIDELINES.

Before classroom management can begin, a teacher must first have a job. The following suggestions are offered to assist new teachers in finding a teaching position and preparing for the first day of school.

1. During your student teaching semester, contact local school districts for application forms. Complete the forms and start sending specified requirements such as fingerprints, letters of recommendation, transcripts, NTE scores, health records, etc. Inquire of the secretary how vacancies are posted and when.

2. Write a resume (Example 2-A) and develop a teaching portfolio (Example 2-B).

3. Attend a college employment conference. THIS IS NOT THE PLACE TO USE A TEACHING PORTFOLIO. Meet with several school districts for the experience of interviewing.

4. Sign up to substitute in schools or offer volunteer services. The key is to get principals to know you and your abilities. Also, this will assist you in learning a school system and its personnel. School contacts will make you more aware of upcoming temporary or permanent vacancies in the school district.

5. Visit school principals. Call for an appointment to discuss your qualifications and job possibilities. Principals can make no promises at this time, but it is important that they see your face. Remember that they are very busy and some may tell you to wait or that it is against district policy to meet with applicants without an authorization from the district personnel office. If so, respect their requests. Be sure to make a follow up call or send a thank you letter after any visit. The use of a portfolio will be very helpful when meeting with principals.

6. Always follow up on any leads. Talk to teachers, friends, and relatives about any teaching positions of which they are aware.

7. Some districts have a job fair or designated day that all applicants meet with principals and/or personnel staff for interviews, and attendance on these days may be mandatory. Once the pool of applicants has been determined, individuals are called to meet with individual principals at various school locations. If you have done your homework, hopefully this will be the second time some of these principals have seen your face. It is not unrealistic to ask to observe classes, tour the school, see the student restrooms, or visit the library. Questions during any of the sessions are generally very situational (What would you do if . . .?). Often more than one person will be in the interview such as other teachers, the counselor, or assistant principals. Always follow up with a call or note.

Once you have been called and offered a position by the principal or personnel director, it is not necessary for you to immediately respond. At least spend one evening weighing the pros and cons of the job. Talk to family, former teachers, and friends regarding your decision. REMEMBER, IT IS NOT NECESSARY TO ACCEPT THE FIRST OFFER THAT COMES ALONG. SOME NEW TEACHERS IN THEIR HASTE FOR A PAYCHECK FAIL TO CONSIDER THE WHOLE PICTURE AND BECOME DISILLUSIONED WITH TEACHING. Another point to remember is that some districts do not hire teachers until August and September for various reasons. Do not get discouraged if you do not have a teaching position by July 1. It may be August 31 or later before you know if there is a place for you in a school district.

REFLECTION

1. Have you completed all necessary paper work with state teacher licensure office?

2. What teaching alternatives do you have if you do not meet all certification requirements?

3. Are you involved in activities now that will add to your resume? If so, list them. If not, list some things that you can do to increase your qualifications.

4. List items that you have done which would be appropriate for a teaching portfolio.

5. *If you plan to leave the state, have you checked with the state department there to verify requirements for a teaching certificate? If yes, what will you need to do?*

6. *Where would you like to teach? Identify at least 3 schools and analyze the pros and cons of each situation.*

7. *Would you be willing to teach in an area or at a grade level outside of your certification? If so, what areas or grade levels?*

Writing a Resume

A resume is important to the job search since it quickly conveys the qualifications, capabilities, and achievements of the applicant. Resumes should be typed on a good quality of neutral colored paper. Remember that your resume is your calling card, and it should be error free and "reader friendly." Usually, the length is about 2 pages.

The elements of a resume are as follows:
1. A cover letter
2. Name, address, phone number and social security number
3. Professional objective
4. Education
5. Student Teaching
6. Experience
      Related
      Unrelated
7. Activities
8. Honors/awards
9. Interests
10. References

For a sample resume for a beginning teacher, see EXAMPLE 2-A.

SAMPLE 2 - A

Elizabeth J. Smith
111 Klondike Dr.
Podunk, Somestate 00000
(000) 222-2222
SS #000-00-0000

Professional Objective	A position in a high school utilizing my academic knowledge and teaching experience.
Education 1995	B. A., Podunk University, Podunk, Somestate Major: English Education Certification: English (7-12) 　　　　　　　　　Journalism (7-12) GPA: 3.7 NTE: Completed December, 1994
Student Teaching	Podunk High School, Podunk, Somestate Under supervision, planned and taught lessons in English I, II, and III
Related Experience 1993 - 95	Camp Counselor, YMCA. Worked with after school care children ages 6-12.
Other Experience	Salesperson and waitress. Used communication and interpersonal skills.
Activities	Member, Kappa Delta Pi Member, National Council Teachers of English Member, First Baptist Church
Honors/Awards	Dean's List (1993-96) Honor's Scholarship Outstanding English Teacher Education Graduate

Interests   Reading, travel, storytelling, basketball

References   **Mrs. Cooperating Teacher**
                                 English Department
                                 Podunk High School
                                 Podunk, Somestate 00000
                                 (000) 888-8888

                                 Dr. University Supervisor
                                 Department of Teacher Education
                                 Podunk University
                                 Podunk, Somestate 00000
                                 (000) 111-1111

                                 Dr. Former Instructor
                                 Department of English
                                 Podunk University
                                 Podunk, Somestate 00000
                                 (000) 555-5555

Activity 2 - A

Instructions: In the space provided, write your resume. Circle the areas in which you need improvement.

The Teaching Portfolio

Below are a list of suggested items to be included in a teaching portfolio. Usually, these artifacts are kept in transparent plastic cover sheets and organized in a three ring binder. For more information about teaching portfolios, read the article "Developing and Using Portfolios" by Betty Jo Simmons on the following page.

Personal philosophy of education - about 1 page, typed

Resume - 2 pages typed

Transcripts

NTE scores (if applicable)

Sample lesson plans

Sample tests

Student assessment plan (formal and informal)

Classroom management plan

Supervisory assessments
   University supervisor
   Cooperating teacher
   Principal

Letters of recommendation

Teaching certificate

Pictures of classroom activities

Certificates of special training

Video of instruction

Self-assessment outlining strengths and areas for improvement

Developing and Using Portfolios

Artists have long used portfolios as a means of displaying their unique talents and accomplishments. Traditionally, teachers also have kept work samples to show the progress and ongoing development of their students. Schools and colleges are now beginning to make frequent use of portfolios for course and program assessment. The purposes for making portfolios are many and differ from one person to another, however, the concept of portfolio development has recently become more formalized and more widely accepted as a valid approach in determining competence levels. Employers, in particular, want to know they are hiring the best available applicant when jobs are offered. Thus, they are requiring more preliminary information to guarantee that the person selected will be able to perform the assigned duties well (Stemmer, Brown, and Smith 1992). The portfolio is the kind of instrument needed to provide this evidence of employability. Portfolios help to move one forward professionally because they serve as a repository for documenting and developing skills along prescribed guidelines (Cleary 1992).

The purpose of this article is to discuss some guidelines for making and using the professional portfolio as a self-evaluation and marketing tool. The focus will be directed primarily toward those who are seeking employment as classroom teachers. The idea presented, therefore, can be easily modified to fit the needs of those who may be seeking jobs in fields outside of education.

Developing Portfolios

Portfolio developers must select approaches that will allow them to make their individual identities clear and that portray them as being uniquely suited for the job. Marsh and Lasky (1984) suggested that a portfolio can become a way to describe one's professional, educational and personal achievements. Actually, this description provides a very logical organizational framework. Developers will do well to begin with a description of who they are professionally, including statements of professional beliefs, philosophy, and goals. They should also provide narrative descriptions of their professional activities, workshops, conferences, organization, and other school-related involvement (such as classroom volunteer experiences, tutorial experiences, substitute teaching, etc.). Developers need to make a direct connection between educational preparation and what will be required on the job. Areas such as planning for instruction, meeting the challenges of diversity, maximizing instructional time, using developmentally appropriate strategies, creating affective classroom climates, and working cooperatively with parents might be highlighted.

At the personal level, developers should include some autobiographical data about how they arrived at their decision to teach and about who they are as individuals. They should discuss previous work experiences that show they can handle responsibility and perform well. The personal section also provides an opportunity to display certificates of merit, honor, and/or accomplishment. For example, having received a certificate in CPR, lifeguarding, first aid, or nonviolent crisis intervention can be especially advantageous when working with children.

Professional Data

Wise portfolio designers will prepare thorough and thoughtful resumes in which educational background, previous employment, job goals, professional affiliations, and other significant achievements are documented. If placement files are available from the college or university career office, they also should be mentioned in the resume. Other important sources of professional information that should be included are transcripts, recommendations, and evaluations. Copies of professional certificates, most notably, a teaching license and last results from the National Teachers examination, along with transcripts of collegiate-level work are vital components. Recommendations from professors and others who are familiar with the academic, leadership, and personal qualities of those making portfolios are important to prospective employers. Likewise, evaluations from early field experiences, student teaching, and internships are invaluable. Interviewers are especially interested in these as proof of how well students actually perform in the classroom as they begin to relate theory to practice in real situations.

Educational Data

Portfolio designers should present evidence that they possess the competencies that most directly align with the types of responsibilities for which they will be held accountable in the performance of the specific job to which they aspire. For those wishing to become classroom teachers, copies of daily unit and block planning should be included. Suggestion for materials to use in this section are tests, items analyses, examples of authentic assessment. IEP development, case studies, work samples from key classes, specimens of handwriting and issues or position papers.

Perhaps the most important component of this section is a videotaped mini-lesson. Portfolio developers should remember to keep their lessons short because interviewers have neither time for nor interest in watching an hour-long presentation. Selecting an objective and addressing it for five minutes, making sure to include as many principles of effective teaching as possible, is a sensible plan of action. Under the educational data section, developers may wish to include some photographs of learning centers, bulletin boards, or special projects. While a few well-chosen pictures can add zest to portfolios, care must be exercised so that portfolios do not take on the nature of a scrapbook.

Personal Data

When constructing a portfolio, developers must be certain that the results set them apart from others in unique ways. Therefore, each person should select the most individually appropriate means for accomplishing this goal. First, a high-quality photograph is helpful. A picture of the developer can become an asset in helping interviewers recall a particular candidate. Second, it is useful to include a carefully constructed autobiography that details pertinent information about the life and the interests of the portfolio developer. In the autobiography, it is a good idea to mention how the decision was made to pursue education as a profession. People or events that affected the decision, are relevant topics for discussion.

Third, it seems logical to include a carefully thought-out philosophy statement. This makes articulation of one's philosophy during an interview much easier. Finally, portfolio developers may select additional personal information that is appropriate for inclusion in this section. Among the possibilities are descriptions of volunteer experiences (particularly those relating to children); narrative information about scholarships, awards, honors; contributions to community affairs; and individual art, music, and literary talents. Naturally, original pieces of work that have been recognized for publication or as being professionally significant enhance employment prospects.

Packaging Portfolios

Portfolio construction is certainly important. However, as Vavrus (1990) said, the most essential consideration is what is inside the container, not the container itself. Yet, failure to give portfolios a professional appearance may result in their receiving less attention than their contents actually merit. Therefore, it is important to select containers that communicate seriousness of purpose, dignity, and good taste. Nice loose-leaf binders are an excellent way to package portfolios because they allow one to add and delete information. They are also easy to handle during an interview.

Developers should have a table of contents followed by tabs, which allow for quick location of a particular piece of data. Orderly arrangement will make portfolios simple to use during interview and will also permit interviewers to access desired information immediately. Neatness is crucial. (The pages of the portfolio should be placed in transparent covers to prevent them from becoming soiled and rumpled.) Likewise, spelling, grammar, and punctuation must be flawless.

Using Portfolios

Portfolios are intended to involve developers in their own learning, self-assessment, and analysis of accomplishments (Burden and Byrd 1994). As a result, they become valuable tools for empowerment and for building self-esteem (Wasserstein 1994). The use of portfolios for personal evaluation is of primary importance, and portfolio development is continuous and ever-changing (Valencia 1990). The fact that portfolios focus upon processes as well as products makes them ideal for marketing purposes. Developers are required to review, analyze, and document their performance. In this process they learn to identify skills they have acquired, knowledge they have gained, and values they believe to be important. This type of exercise then enables them to become naturally conversant in these areas. Consequently, portfolio developers give themselves a tremendous edge in preparing for interviews. Simultaneously, portfolios give interviewers an advantage because the structured components that make up portfolios allow immediate and selective pursuit of areas where pertinent in-depth information is desired (James and Van Cleaf 1990).

Interviewees must politely, but aggressively make sure their portfolios are used in strategic ways during the interviews. For example, an interview opening with a commonly used general statement like "tell me something about yourself" affords the interviewee the perfect opportunity to produce the portfolio. Candidates must take every opportunity to make their portfolios very visible, to share the contents, and to be prepared to access information quickly (Bowling Green Kappa Delta Pi 1990).

The burden rests with applicants to impress upon those in hiring positions that a wealth of material is within a hand's reach. This means applicants must be thoroughly familiar with the organization of their portfolios and must practice using them to avoid looking awkward and uncomfortable locating materials during the interview. Indeed, having the information collected and ready for presentation should greatly bolster candidates' confidence levels and improve their chances of making a first-rate

impression. Skillful portfolio usage will enable candidates to present themselves as organized, well-prepared, and poised.

Before leaving the interview, candidates should offer to leave their portfolios for a few days, giving the interviewer more time to peruse the contents. Candidates should call attention to videotapes included in their portfolios by inviting the interviewer to look at an actual teach episode. Candidates should retrieve their portfolios at a mutually arranged time.

Even if they are assured of a contract, candidates should ask to have their portfolios returned because they must continue the development process after they have been employed. Developers who continuously add work samples from their classrooms, ideas for innovative teaching, and other evidence of professional merit will have portfolios that will serve as ideal tools for validating on-the-job success.

Summary

As a systematic, purposeful collection of work and accomplishments, portfolios give developers the chance to showcase their efforts, progress, and ultimate achievements (Paulson, Paulson, and Meyer 1991). Portfolios have myriad uses: however, they are especially well-suited for marketing oneself as a professional because they require huge amounts of reflection, self-evaluation, and organization. The contents can contain whatever developers wish as a means of showing growth in understandings, skills, and goal attainment (Worthen, Borg, and White 1993). Portfolios provide assessment both in terms of process and product. As a result, developers become adept at persuading others of their level of expertise (Brownell 1993). They feel challenged, empowered, and affirmed as they capture and share their experiences. Portfolio developers learn to put themselves "out front," providing unique, interesting, and coherent, supportive documentation of their professional competence.

References

Bowling Green Kappa Delta Pi. 1990. Marketing yourself as a professional. Bowling Green, Ohio; Bowling Green State University Kappa Delta Pi.

Brownell, J. 1993 Dealing in diamonds; Writing that works. Delta Kappa Gamma Bulletin 60-1 c 43-48.

Burden, P., and D. Byrd, 1994. Methods for effective teaching Needham Heights, Mass.: Allyn & Bacon.

Cleary, M. 1992. Giving professional preparation an occupational focus. Journal of Health Education 23(5): 314-15.

James, A. and D. Van Cleaf, 1990. Portfolios for preservice teachers. Kappa Delta Pi Record 26(2): 43-45.

Marsh, H., and P. Lasky, 1984. The professional portfolio: Documentation of prior learning. Nursing Outlook 32(5): 264-67.

Paulson, F., P. Paulson, and C. Meyer, 1991. What makes a portfolio a portfolio? Educational Leadership 46-5: 50-53.

Stemmer, P., B. Brown and C. Smith, 1992. The employability skills portfolio. Educational Leadership 49 6 32.

Valencia, S. 1990. A portfolio approach to classroom assessment. The Reading Teacher 43-4 336-40.

Vavrus, L. 1990. Put portfolios to the test. Instructor 100 (1) 45-53.

Wasserstein, P. 1994. To do or not to do portfolios. That is the question. Kappa Delta Pi Record 31 1r. 12-15

Worthen, B., W. R. Borg. and K. R. White, 1993. Measurement and evaluation in the schools. White Plains, N. Y.: Longman.

Author

Betty Jo Simmons is Associate Processor of Education at Longwood College in Farmville, Virginia. She teaches classes in educational evaluation and methods of instruction and supervises student teachers. Dr. Simmons serves on a local school board, and is the Counselor of Beta Epsilon Chapter of Kappa Delta Pi at Longwood College.

Countdown

Before students actually enter your classroom, there are many things to learn about your school system, its personnel, and its daily business procedures so that you as a new teacher feel confident and prepared for the first day of school. The following checklist is designed to help you begin your management program. Some of the information listed can be found in the faculty handbook or through interviews with the principal, secretary, and other personnel. All items listed on the countdown sheet should be checked before the beginning of school.

 TWO MONTHS BEFORE SCHOOL

___ 1. Visit the school and get copies of textbooks, teacher's guides, and workbooks. If class rosters are available, ask for yours.

___ 2. Look at the curriculum guide (state and/or local) to determine general instructional goals, scope and sequence, and activities related to these.

___ 3. Develop an outline of specific concepts to cover over the school year.

___ 4. Obtain a list of resources available at the school and at the district media center. Inquire how to arrange for the use of these resources.

___ 5. Get a copy of the bell schedule.

___ 6. Get a copy of the school map. Locate duplication areas, storage rooms, book rooms, fire extinguishers, student records, AV equipment, lost and found, faculty restrooms, and special service rooms such as music, resource, and art.

___ 7. Get a copy of the school calendar. Identify on a master calendar holidays, assembly days, testing days, and faculty meeting days. Purchase a personal calendar to keep in your possession with special days identified.

___ 8. Develop a resource file of volunteers and special services offered to the school through special programs. Make a list of contact persons with phone numbers and addresses.

___ 9. Get a copy of the dress code for faculty and students.

___10. Begin to plan your wardrobe for the school year.

___11. Ask for a mentor. Once assigned, call and make an appointment to meet with him/her.

___12. As you read the text, record your readings on tapes, label, and use as a supplement for students. Place them on reserve in the library, create a reading center, or check them out to students yourself.

___13. Read a copy of the school's philosophy.

___14. Collect shoe boxes, coffee cans, etc. to store materials and supplies.

___15. Make a list of reports and records you must keep and identify forms, format, and due dates.

___16. Inquire if report cards are computer generated or hand written.

___17. Visit the district media center. Develop a list of materials and services there. Meet the media specialist and inquire of workshops related to media use.

___18. Make an appointment to visit with the curriculum specialist for the district. Inquire about banned books, curriculum flexibility, grade level expectations, services, etc.

___19.

___20.

SIX WEEKS BEFORE SCHOOL

___ 1. Visit your classroom.

___ 2. Develop an inventory list of books, materials, and furniture in the room and file for future reference.

___ 3. Inquire about supplies. What are you expected to purchase? Is there available money from various groups such as PTO?

___ 4. Become acquainted with the faculty, support personnel, and staff of the school. Learn their names and titles, and if possible, visit with them.

___ 5. Document special school services such as after school care, breakfast programs, free lunch programs, etc. Identify contact persons with phone numbers.

___ 6. Develop a list of your specific responsibilities related to duty, reporting absentees and tardies, extracurricular activities, committee membership, PTO, money collection, and fund raising.

___ 7. Become familiar with the district/school discipline policy.

___ 8. Make a list of rules related to the lunchroom, restroom, tardy admissions, and school bus.

___ 9. Meet with the principal or his/her designee to discuss policies related to excused and unexcused absences, sick or injured students, classroom parties, and field trips. Make notations.

___ 10. Read, highlight, and define your responsibilities related to dress code for students.

___ 11. Learn about the specific lesson plan format recommended by the district, the due date of lesson plans to the office, and the person who is your supervisor.

___ 12. Identify the policy for your own absences (personal days and sick days) and the procedure for selecting a substitute.

___ 13. Examine the cumulative records for your students.

___ 14. Study the attendance area of the school district and note specifics such as average family income, businesses, employment opportunities, etc.

___15. Ask the secretary about personal telephone calls and mail.

___16. Locate your faculty box.

___17. Identify the chain of command with names, locations, and phone numbers.

___18. Identify members of the School Building Level Committee and the procedure to follow for referrals.

___19. From your class roster, have the counselor or special education teacher identify mainstreamed or included students. Ask to see the Individual Educational Plan (IEP) for each student if it involves your classroom instruction. If the student qualifies for accommodations under 504, ask for specific strategies to use (Example 2-c).

___20. Visit garage sales and goodwill organizations to buy paperbacks, games, shelving, generic shirts/shorts, curtains, etc. for the classroom.

___21. Identify students with religious affiliations that may require them to miss school days or prevent them from participating in various activities.

___22. Develop a resource file of places and people considered to be community resources for classroom enrichment.

___23. Meet the janitors. Learn their names.

___24. Inquire as to the procedure for requesting classroom furniture, books, and media. Make formal requests for "extras" in your classroom.

___25. Meet with the secretary to find out any expectations he/she may have of you.

___26. Meet with the counselor to discuss any personal problems that your students may be facing.

___27. Identify special counseling services and programs for students.

___28. Post copies of evacuation procedures. Identify exits and locations of fire extinguishers.

___29. Inquire of the principal how your personal performance evaluations will be conducted.

___30. Determine if you will be required to go through state assessment for new teachers. If so, who makes up your committee?

Example 2-C

DOCUMENTATION OF APPROPRIATE INDIVIDUAL INTERVENTION STRATEGIES

STUDENT: _____ SEMESTER/YEAR: _____

COURSE#/SECTION: _____ INSTRUCTOR: _____

INSTRUCTIONAL ACCOMMODATIONS AND MODIFICATIONS							
Check those recommended and star those which are successful for this student.							
Indicate the date the intervention began.							
DATE	✔	•					
			INSTRUCTION				
			Extra coaching during office hours				
			Multisensory approaches				
			Directions given in more than one way				
			Repeating/paraphrasing information				
			Variety of teaching methods				
			Shortened, modified, taped, or fewer assignments				
			Clearly stated daily objectives				
			PARTICIPATION				
			Increased response time				
			Preferential seating				
			Rest time				
			Detailed instruction sheets for assignments				
			Advanced notice of class discussions and activities				
			ORGANIZATION/STUDY SKILLS				
			Peer assistance in notetaking, assignments				
			Taped textbooks				
			Highlighted textbooks				
			Taped lectures				
			Photocopied teacher notes				
			Wide ruled notebooks				
			Study groups				
			Review sheets/class review				
			Lesson outlines				
			Use of mnemonic devices				
			Advance notice of assignments				
			READING				
			Highlighted textbooks				
			Colored film overlays				
			Softer lighting				
			Pre-reading questions				
			Taped textbooks				
			Advanced notice of reading assignments				
			WRITING				
			Allow for misspelled words				
			Extra time				
			Shorten assignments				
			Use of lap top computers with spell check				
			Write "orally" in tape player, transcribe, edit				
			Check rough draft/allow student to read paper to you				
			Writing portfolio				
			TEST TAKING				
			Read direction to students				
			Extended time				
			Test type(s)				
			Grouping of test items				
			Typed tests with large print				
			Test options for orally taping answers or an oral test				
			Less stressful location for testing				
			OTHERS				

ONE MONTH BEFORE SCHOOL

___ 1. Develop a floor plan of your classroom and arrange furniture and learning centers accordingly.

___ 2. Determine the types of learning centers for your classroom and begin to collect needed materials such as tables, boxes, crates, etc.

___ 3. Collect plastic grocery bags to use as individual garbage holders.

___ 4. Hang posters, maps, pictures, etc.

___ 5. Complete functional bulletin boards. Create an appealing environment for learning.

___ 6. Develop games and activities for classroom instruction.

___ 7. Complete the first 2 weeks of lesson plans including copies, activities, enrichment activities, materials, etc. Make written request for needed materials for these two weeks.

___ 8. Develop a sequence of routines for the class such as returning papers, sharpening pencils, etc.

___ 9. Hang a poster of your classroom rules, rewards, and consequences in a location visible to all students.

___10. From the office, acquire multiple copies of standard forms such as referral slips, admit slips, interim reports, etc.

___11. Develop your "Access to Excess" file for students (a place for extra handouts, etc.)

___12. Review the grading policy of the district and modify your evaluation process to conform with the school.

___13. Develop a policy regarding late work, make-up work, extra credit, and homework checks.

___14. Prepare an introductory letter to parents to be mailed or disseminated the first day of school (Example 2-D).

___15. Make a folder for each student in your class. Determine the location of these folders based on student or teacher use. Often two folders are required.

___16. Make multiple copies of roster sheets with columns to indicate payment of school fees, textbook number, etc.

___17. Plan to use temporary rosters for attendance and grading for at least three weeks until rosters are finalized (Example 2-E).

___18. Develop a school supply list and request local merchants to post it. Remember that you should not penalize a student for failure to purchase school supplies. Make your list realistic, and do not require non-educational related supplies such as tissue, paper towels, and grading pens.

___19. Purchase 5 extra sets of classroom supplies required of students.

___20. Identify the designated person or organization to report accidents, suspicioned child abuse, or student conduct.

___21. Post samples of tests, report headings/format, notebooks, and homework assignments.

___22. Identify the duties of a homeroom teacher.

___23.

Example 2-D
Sample Letter to Parents

Dear Mr. and Mrs. _____,

    I am very pleased to have _____ in my class this year. We can all look forward to a very progressive year filled with exciting learning activities.

    So that every student in the classroom can reach his/her potential in a positive educational climate, it is important that each student demonstrate self-discipline. To encourage a cooperative academic environment, the following classroom rules were developed:

        One voice at a time.
        Keep hands and feet to yourself.
        Respect others and their property.

    Any student who breaks a rule will first receive a warning. The second time, the student will be detained at lunch recess for 15 minutes to discuss the breaking of the rule(s). The third time, the student will be detained at lunch until a meaningful punishment has been completed. The fourth time will result in a parent/teacher conference. If the misbehavior continues, the student will be referred to the office or counselor.

    Homework is necessary to reinforce a concept learned during classtime. Usually, students will have 30 - 45 minutes of homework two or three times each week. In addition, extra study time for tests, projects, etc. will be required. A monthly calendar will be sent home with test dates and project due dates. If a student has an excused absence, it is his/her responsibility to make-up all classwork, homework, tests, and projects within five school days of the return to class. Any work not completed during this time will result in a grade of zero.

    All students have been informed of the classroom rules, homework policy, and make up policy. I would appreciate it if you would review the plan with your child and then sign and return the attached form. Please feel free to contact me at any time. You may reach me at home (000-0000) or call the school (111-1111) for a conference.

    I look forward to working with you and your child this school year.

                 Sincerely,

                 John Smith

_____

I have read your classroom rules, homework policy, and make-up policy and have discussed it with my child, _____.

_____   _____

Parent's Signature   Date

Comments:

Example 2 - E

Temporary Rosters

| | | PERIOD BEGINNING _____ 19 ____ |
| _____ | | PERIOD ENDING _____ 19 ____ |

MONTH																									
DATE																									
NAMES		M	T	W	T	F	M	T	W	T	F	M	T	W	T	F	M	T	W	T	F	M	T	W	
	1																								
	2																								
	3																								
	4																								
	5																								
	6																								
	7																								
	8																								
	9																								
	10																								
	11																								
	12																								
	13																								
	14																								
	15																								
	16																								
	17																								
	18																								
	19																								
	20																								
	21																								
	22																								
	23																								
	24																								
	25																								
	26																								
	27																								
	28																								
	29																								
	30																								
	31																								
	32																								
	33																								
	34																								
	35																								

TWO WEEKS BEFORE SCHOOL

___ 1. Design name plates or tags for students.

___ 2. Designate board or wall space for homework assignments and daily objectives.

___ 3. Develop a seating chart.

___ 4. Post your name and room number outside of your classroom visible for students.

___ 5. Pack a bag of personal needs to include a "generic" shirt/blouse, skirt/pants, socks/panty hose, make-up, aspirins, band-aids, toothbrush, etc.

___ 6. Start a substitute folder with a minimum of three lesson plans with activities and student copies. You should include a class roster and seating chart along with the names and accommodations of any special students.

___ 7. Prepare enrichment activities such as puzzles, music, art, logic problems, etc.

___ 8. Turn in to the office your first complete set of lesson plans.

___ 9. Purchase personal desk needs such as pens, paper, file labels, stapler, etc.

___10. Determine if there are limits on xeroxing materials.

___11. Attend all in-service training for new teachers.

___12.

___13.

ONE WEEK BEFORE SCHOOL

___ 1. Modify the classroom environment to meet needs of various learners.

___ 2. Plan your lesson for introducing classroom procedures and rules.

___ 3. Continue to plan lessons for the third and fourth weeks of class. Your goal is to stay at least two weeks ahead.

___ 4. Meet with at least 5 veteran teachers and make a list of their suggestions.

___ 5. Develop or obtain from the office standardized parent conference sheets.

___ 6. Store safely at least 5 days of lunch money.

___ 7. Sharpen pencils.

___ 8. Prepare take home packets for students which include a student welcome letter, a list of needed school supplies, an explanation of classroom rules, rewards, and consequences, a copy of the grading policy, insurance forms, information cards, a description of the attendance and tardy policies, student handbook, etc. Include a form for parents and students to sign indicating they have received and read the contents of the packet. Place the packets on students' desks.

___ 9. Continue to decorate your classroom with attractive materials and plants.

___10. Number books and write students' names in the texts. Place the assigned books on each student's desk. Be sure to use your seating chart.

___11. Sign out equipment such as tape players and overhead projectors for the year.

___12. Inquire as to whether of not the school supplies attendance books and a grade books. If not, purchase them. Note specific requirements for documenting grades and attendance.

___13. Thoroughly clean the classroom. Dust shelves, clean the chalk board, etc.

___14.

THE DAY BEFORE SCHOOL

___ 1. Check through the list of planning activities. Address any items not completed.

___ 2. Review plans for the first day of class.

___ 3. Inspect the classroom for the last time for organization, attractiveness, and cleanliness.

___4. Put student name plates and/or tags on designated seats.

___ 5. Make last minutes changes to the class roster.

___ 6. Write your name, room number, and tomorrow's date on the board. Put chalk and erasers out. Set up any AV equipment you will need.

___ 7. Put on your desk all needed materials such as a roster, student packet, lesson plans, a list of routines to teach students, etc.

___ 8. If everything is prepared, GO HOME AND REST!

THE FIRST DAY OF SCHOOL

_____ 1. Arrive at school early and allow yourself some quiet time before students arrive.

_____ 2. Have seating assignments clearly posted.

_____ 3. Greet all students at the door by name. Check schedules to verify they are in the right room. Direct students to their desks.

_____ 4. Set the tone for the rest of the year. Begin class as soon as the bell rings.

_____ 5. Introduce yourself. Your name should be on the board. Tell students a little bit about yourself.

_____ 6. Call roll.

_____ 7. Complete all school announcements and business

_____ 8. Teach at least one classroom routine.

_____ 9. Complete at least one academic activity. Do not allow "free time" for students to talk.

_____10. YOU dismiss the class at the appropriate time.

A Teacher's Shopping List

Your new classroom will need several items for a variety of planned as well as unexpected daily events. Consider the following "shopping list" when supplying your classroom.

****

5 sets of student school supplies (for those who can't afford to purchase them)
bucket
mop/broom
dust cloth/rags
cleaning liquid
cleanser
polish
sawdust/sand
used textbooks
file folders
index cards
postage stamps
paper
pens
pencils
stapler/staples
paper clips
grade book/attendance book
generic clothes items for students
cosmetic needs
panty hose
personal hygiene needs
5 three-ring binders
shelving (if needed)
5 sheets of poster paper
construction paper
scissors
name tags
felt pens
safety pins
aspirin (for the teacher)
band aids
antacids (for the teacher)
breath freshener
toothbrush/paste
curling iron
brush/comb

trays for incoming and outgoing
storage bins (if needed)
paper towels
kleenex
three-hole punch
ruler
stencils
briefcase or bag
pot plants
enrichment activities such as puzzle books, etc.
rubber bands
thumb tacs
push pins
white out correction fluid
scotch tape
masking tape
radio
transparent contact paper
file box for index cards
pictures or wall hangings
desk calendar
wall calendar
posters
air freshener
2 timers
extension cord
flashlight
overhead bulb
hammer
screwdriver
bobby pins
chalk
transparencies
transparency markers
clock
tapes - audio and video
glue gun and sticks
needle and thread
straight pins
velcro
magnetic tape
two-sided tape
staple remover
sticky tack
clothespins

whistle
spray bottle
baby wipes
garbage bags
ziploc bags (assorted sizes)
post-it notes
signature stamp
batteries (assorted sizes)
toothpicks
straight edged razor blades
brads
Q-tips
receipt book
matches
knife
iron
measuring tape
plastic storage crates
pencil holder

Student Supply Lists

Preparing a school supply list is a hard task for new teachers. What items and materials will students need to enhance their learning? Should there be only one list per grade or subject for all teachers? What about the expense of the items?

Some things to keep in mind when preparing your list are:

1. Be specific as to quantity (1 pack (500 sheets) of loose leaf paper)
2. Limit items to essentials related to academics. This means NO paper towels, tissue, red pens, etc.
3. Keep cost to a minimum.
4. Post copies of the list at various store locations about 6 weeks prior to the opening of school if possible.

Activity 2 - B

Instructions: On the next several pages are actual school supply lists of teachers from various grade levels. Analyze each list. Mark through those things that are inappropriate for a school supply list, and rewrite general items to make them more specific. Be prepared to justify your answers. Take one of the lists to a local store and estimate the cost.

Kindergarten

Boys: 1 pkg. of brown or white lunch bags; 1 box (quart size) Zip Lock bags
Girls: 1 pkg. of inexpensive white paper plates; 1 box (pint size) Zip Lock bags
1 tote bag or back pack
4 plain pocket folders (no clasps, no names, solid colors)
2 pocket folders with clasps (solid color, no names)
1 dozen #2 yellow pencils
2 boxes of crayons
1 box broad tip Crayola Markers (classic colors)
2 yellow highlighter markers
2 packs of novelty stickers
Change of clothes including socks and underwear. Label with the child's name.
1 nap mat

Third Grade

1 tote bag or back pack

plastic school box with snap fasten top (cigar box size only - no handle)

6 spiral notebooks (wide rule) - 2 red, 2 blue, 1 green, and 1 yellow.

2 pkg. of loose leaf paper (wide rule)

2 doz #2 pencils

1 pkg of 3X5 notecards

1 box fine tip washable markers

1 box broad tip washable markers

2 yellow highlighters

1 pkg. of novelty stickers

4 blue pens

1 12" ruler (centimeters and inches)

1 box (20 ct.) of Zip Lock bags

1 pkg of colored pencils, sharpened

4 pocket folders with clasps (1 yellow, 1 blue, 1 green, 1 red)

1 composition notebook (black and white cover)

1 pair fiskar scissors

1 glue stick

1 Webster's New World Dictionary (available at _____)

1 Spanish Dictionary

1 covered pencil sharpener

2 pks. 3X3 Post It notes

3 pks. of multicolored modeling clay

Third Grade*

10 spiral notebooks - do not label
8 folders with pockets and brads
Pencils
Red marking pencils or pens
1 ruler with metric and inches
Multiplication flashcards
Division flashcards
4 pks of 3X5 index cards
Loose leaf paper (wide rule)
Crayons
Safety scissors
Construction paper - 1 pack of asst. colors and 1 pack of white
Elmer's glue
Crayola markers
Supply Box
2 manilla folders
1 3X5 file box
1 box of tissue
1 pkg. of colored pencils
1 roll paper towels

*Individual teachers will give your child a list of any additional supplies on the first day of school.

Sixth Grade

5 spiral notebooks
1 pks of loose leaf notebook paper
1 notebook binder
1 pack construction paper
2 pocket folders with brads
1 marker set
1 bottle cement glue
1 scotch tape
1 stapler and staples
scissors
blue pens and red pens
pencils
2 boxes of Kleenex
2 rolls of paper towels
1 dictionary
1 thesaurus
1 watercolor set

Ninth Grade

6 five subject notebooks
loose leaf paper
reinforcement rings
2 pocket folders
6 manila folders
2 black pens
3 red pens
10 pencils
collegiate dictionary
thesaurus
1 three ring binder - hard cover
3 textbook covers
1 pkg. of graphing paper
Scotch tape
colored pencils
tissue

THE SUPPLY FEE FOR 19__ - 19__ WILL BE $10.00.

Activity 2 - C

Instructions: Think about the grade(s) you would like to teach. Develop a student supply list that you consider essential to an organized school beginning. Estimate the cost.

Reflection

1. How can school supplies discriminate against students?

2. In your classroom, will students keep their own supplies or will you create a "community" supply system? Justify your answer.

3. How will you provide for those students who can not afford to purchase school supplies?

4. What are some possible sources for student supplies and/or money for supplies?

Quick Tip
Basics of Interviewing

Things that impress potential employers:
- be on time
- dress appropriately
- give a firm handshake
- don't chatter, smoke, chew gum, or fidget
- speak with enthusiasm and assurance
- be positive
- give thought to questions before answering
- have a basic knowledge of the position
- have questions to ask the interviewer

Common mistakes made when interviewing:
- lack of enthusiasm
- appearing too anxious, nervous, or cocky
- talking too much, too little, too loudly, too negatively
- being uninformed about the position
- dressing inappropriately
- wearing too much cologne
- arriving late for the interview

For a list of sample interview questions, see the article "Interviewing Teacher Candidates: 100 Questions to Ask" by James E. Ferguson on pages 53-55.

Interviewing Teacher Candidates: 100 Questions to Ask

This list can be used as a resource for developing your own set interview questions.

By James E. Ferguson

Advance preparation is essential to the successful screening of applicants for teaching positions. Further, if all candidates are asked the same questions you will be assured that all candidates are treated equally, and you will have a common base upon which to evaluate applicants.

Listed below are 100 questions that may be asked when interviewing potential teachers. Obviously, it would be impossible to raise all 100 questions in one interview. The list is designed to serve as a resource from which to draw. The interviewer is encouraged to adjust questions to fit the vacancy and the interview.

1. What is your educational preparation? (Cite preparation in content area.)
2. What are your professional experiences?
3. What is the role of the teacher in the classroom?
4. How would you describe your last principal?
5. What was your favorite course in college, and why?
6. What principles do you use to motivate students?
7. Describe effective teaching techniques that result in intended learning.
8. What are your career goal five years from now? Ten years?
9. State a behavioral objective you taught in your last class.
10. What is the most exciting thing happening in the area of education today?
11. What is the most exciting thing happening today in your area of study?
12. What have you found to be the toughest aspect of discipline?
13. Describe the physical appearance of your classroom.
14. Describe an ideal curriculum in your area of study.
16. How do you implement career education concepts in your classes?
17. How do you individualize learning in your classes?
18. Define current curriculum trends in your area.
19. How much do you devote to the lecture approach?
20. Describe independent study projects your students have completed.
21. If you could choose to teach any concept in your area, which would you select? Why?
22. What rules have you established for your classroom?
23. How have you implemented inquiry?
24. Of what use are behavioral learning objectives in the teaching/learning process?
25. How do you structure your class to achieve maximum benefit from teacher/student contact?
26. Describe the format you use to develop a lesson.
27. What should schools do for students?
28. Is the teaching of content important? Why/why not?
29. How have you emphasized the development of basic skills?
30. How do you handle the different ability levels of students in classes?
31. How do you account for the affective domain in your teaching?
32. How would your students describe you?
33. In what professional organizations do you hold membership?
34. How would your colleagues describe you?
35. Why did you choose the teaching profession?

36. How have you recently improved your professional skills?
37. What are your plans for future improvement of professional skills.
38. What is the toughest aspect of teaching today?
39. What is the role of homework?
40. What has been your most positive teaching experience? Negative?
41. How have you contributed toward development of the total school program in your current position?
42. What activities will you sponsor if you are hired for this position?
43. Could a student of low academic ability receive a high grade in your classes?
44. What is your system for evaluating student work?
45. What would be the ideal philosophy of a school for you?
46. What is your philosophy of education?
47. Why is your field important for a student to study?
48. How would you handle a student who is a consistent behavioral problem in your class?
49. How would your last principal describe you?
50. What five words would you use to describe yourself?
51. What is your position on teacher-advisement programs? Behavior modification? Tracking? Special education? Values clarification? Multi-test approach?
52. If you found nonstandard usage in student writing or class discussion, how would you respond to it?
53. In what areas do you feel you need improvement?
54. How would you handle a student sleeping in your class?
55. What would you do if a student has been absent your class for several days?
56. What provisions have you made for the gifted?
57. What would a visitor in your class see?
58. How have you communicated student progress to parents?
59. What are your recreational activities, hobbies, interests?
60. How have you stressed the development of cognitive skills within your classes?
61. Define a superior teacher.
62. What is your opinion of holding students after school for detention?
63. Do you like laughter in your classroom?
64. What units would you include in teaching (name of course)?
65. How do you assist in preventing the destruction of school property in your classroom?
66. What is the role of the student within your classroom?
67. Describe an assignment that you recently gave to your students.
68. Cite the criteria you would use to evaluate a textbook for possible adoption.
69. What field trips have you arranged for your classes during this past year?
70. Have you supervised student teachers, interns, or practicum students? Why/why not?
71. Should sex education be included in the curriculum? Why/why not?
72. Are you well organized?
73. Describe a lesson plan that you have developed? What were the objectives, the format of the lesson, and how did you evaluate whether or not the objectives were achieved?
74. A student tells you he/she has been experimenting with marijuana. What would you do?
75. Should schools practice corporal punishment? Why/why not?
76. Give an example of directions you have given for class or homework.
77. What are your practices in dealing with controversial subjects?
78. How have your classes made use of the library during the last nine weeks?
79. What should your students have gained from having taken your course?
80. What are your strong points?
81. What curricular materials have you developed?
82. How would you change the public schools if you could make any changes you wished?
83. What is your position on competency-based instruction?
84. What do you like most about being a teacher?
85. Which aspects of teaching do you like least?
86. Do you like to have people like you?
87. What time management principles to you follow?
88. How do you cope with stress?
89. What motivates you?
90. Why do you want to leave your present position?
91. How have you involved parents in the learning process?
92. Describe your last workday.
93. If you could, what would you change about your present position?

94.   Name the titles of the last three books that
        you have read.

95.   How many days of work have you missed in
        the last three years?

96.   What two or three books, concepts, or
        experiences have influenced you the
        most in your professional development?

97.   Can a school be too student-oriented?
        Explain.

98.   Why should you be hired?

99.   What questions have I not asked that you
        wished I would have raised?

100.   If you are selected for this position, what can
        we do to help you be successful?

Quick Tip
Time Management

If finding enough time is your problem, follow these suggestions.

1. Think about time.

2. Establish goals.

3. Stay focused.

4. Take time to make time.

5. Use visual aids.

6. Make long range plans.

7. Delegate. Invite parents to serve as an aid in the classroom.

8. Skim reading materials.

9. Take fewer papers home. Use portfolios in grading.

10. Minimize procrastination.

11. Learn to say no.

12. Take time to rejuvenate.

13. Accomplish several tasks simultaneously.

14. Be flexible.

15. Attend only events linked to your priorities.

16. Arrive early and stay late.

17. Observe and conference with other teachers to discover their management plans.

18. Keep a calendar and color code events.

19. Keep a notepad or tape player on your nightstand and in your car.

20. Begin each day with a clear desk.

21. When xeroxing materials, make twice as many for next year. Utilize the chalkboard and transparencies when possible.

22. Assign students numbers and have them record this number on papers. As students pass up papers, have them order numerically.

23. Make several sets of address labels for students for quick notes to be mailed home.

24. Cover bulletin boards with fabric.

25. Laminate bulletin board materials and file for future use.

26. Color code classes and clip papers with the appropriate color.

27. File weekly and have students file their own papers.

28. Make a "to do" list each day.

29. Use worksheets as extensions of mastery.

30. Get rid of your desk if it only collects clutter.

31. Learn to manage mail and advertisements.

32. Require students to peer edit papers. Use student papers for multiple assignments.

33. Assign a supply monitor and a classroom host.

34. Divide the bulletin board into sections and assign different students to decorate that section.

35. Prepare weekly assignment sheets or access to excess

Quick Tip
What Do I Do with Extra Time?

1. Before students leave the room for an assembly, etc., pass out handouts, give page numbers, etc., and tell them exactly what is to be done when the class returns.

2. Play music while students are testing, etc. For early finishers, offer bonus points if they can name the composer and the song title.

3. Using old magazines, have students clip pictures and phrases to develop a cartoon book of their own.

4. Divide the class into two teams. Have a member of Team A come to the front and sit on a stool with his/her back to the board. The teacher writes a word, character, place, etc. above the student's head on the board. Other team members on Team A will then take turns giving one word clues. Points are determined by the number of clues. Once the term has been guessed, Team B tries. The team with the least points wins.

5. Based on the day's lesson, have students write 2-5 questions that could be used on a test.

6. Read to students from high interest books.

7. Make copies of original poems, paragraphs, essays, short stories, etc. that students write. Have students read them to the class when there is extra time. This frees the teacher to prepare for the next class, etc.

8. On a sheet of paper have a series of lines, triangles, squiggles, etc. drawn. Require students to create a picture using these lines. It could be caricatures, etc.

9. Play a game of links. Put several interconnecting circles on the board and write a word in one such as "novel." Then, each student must follow by going to the board and writing a word in the next link related to the previous link.

10. Allow students equal time (1-2 minutes) to voice opinions related to a current issue.

11. On cards, list a variety of commands. Select a student to begin, and read one of the commands. The student performs the command and then calls on someone. A second command is given, and that student must perform the first and second. The game continues until a student can not remember the commands.

12. The Think Tank -- Have several review questions from the current and previous units in a large bowl. Draw a question from the bowl and have members of class teams answer them. Score points with prizes for the winning team.

13. Pin the statement on the map. Using a map of the world or USA, have one sentence descriptions written on pieces of paper. Have students pin the descriptions on the correct map location.

14. Write a series of letters on the board, such as AACDS and have students write a sentence. Example: All apples collected didn't sour. The student with the most sentences wins a prize of some type.

15. On the overhead, show a list of 25 to 50 unrelated words. Allow the students to view for about 1 minute. Remove the list and have students record as many words as possible in the remaining time. Collect lists as students are leaving. The student remembering the most receives a reward.

16. Use flash cards to teach students common words in another language such as Spanish or hand signs for hearing impaired.

17. Draw a large circle on the board. Think of a category such as "health" and write two or three clues inside the circle. Have students guess. Correct answers go inside the circle and incorrect go on the outside. The first student to guess wins.

18. Select two students and have them stand back to back in front of the room. Have other class members develop a list of how they are alike and different.

19. Guess the author. Give students several clues about a writer. Have students guess.

20. Tape several unusual sounds on an audio tape. Have students guess the sound.

21. Select a number from 0 to 1000. Have students ask questions to narrow the range for guessing.

22. Student VIP interviews. Have students write 5 interview questions on a piece of paper. Draw the name of one student to be interviewed. Class will then take turns asking questions of the student. The interview ends and the student must use one word that best describes himself/herself.

23. Have laminated life-size computer keyboard sheets for each student. Teach basic finger positions. Have students practice key board skills as you call out words or sentences.

Chapter 3
Environmental Management

Focus

1. To design a physical classroom layout that promotes effective and efficient instruction.
2. To explore grouping techniques that promote efficient use of time.
3. To identify various types of learning centers for grades K-12.

Reflection

     Many of the things you do prior to the first day of school will determine the type of classroom you will have. New teachers in their haste to buy a grade book and write a list of classroom rules fail to understand the importance of the actual management of the classroom environment. Take a few minutes now to envision your future classroom. Now use at least 10 adjectives to describe its overall appearance.

Physical Room Management

The physical arrangement of the classroom is an important aspect of management. *It is recommended that teachers BEGIN the school year with students seated in straight rows. If tables are used, students should be positioned with chair(s) on two sides of the table to give the appearance of rows.* This seating arrangement will create a more structured first impression for students at the beginning of the school year. Room arrangements and seating charts may be modified throughout the semester as the new teacher learns the individual personalities and needs of the students in the classroom.

Activity 3 - A

Pretend you are a first year teacher planning the room arrangement for your 25 students. Using the graphing sheet on the following page, literally design the floor plan for your classroom using the specifications below:

Student Desk	3X3
Teacher Desk	3X6
Chair	2X2
Table	3X4
Bookcase	1X4X5 or 1X4X3
Storage Closet	3x5
Beanbags	2X2
4 Drawer File	1X3
Podium	2X2
Overhead Cart	2X2

There is no limit to the number of files, bookcases, etc., but keep in mind the necessity for monitoring the classroom. Also on your diagram, identify the locations of maps, screens, clocks, learning centers, pencil sharpeners, and trash cans.

Using a pencil for this activity is recommended.

Activity 3 - A

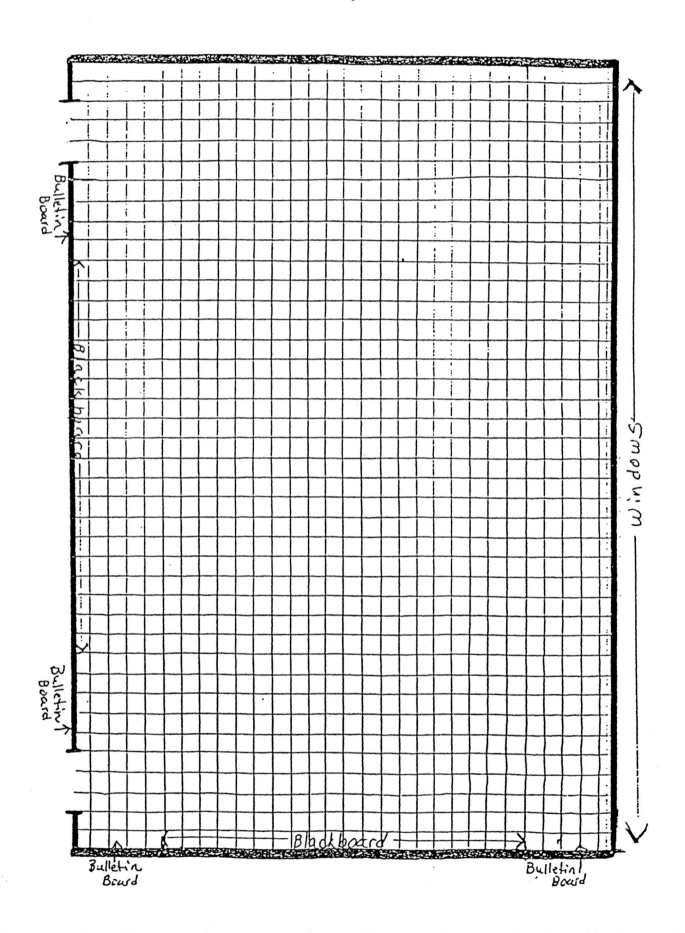

Activity 3 - B

Instructions: In every class there are various student behaviors that could be a potential discipline problem. Sometimes, the mere placement of these students in the classroom serves as a preventive technique. Examine each of the types below and envision their characteristics. Now return to the diagram of your classroom on the previous page and physically place these students in the classroom. Be able to justify your seating choices.

The Class Clown - This student loves to be the comedian of the classroom.

The Derailed Genius - This student is extremely bright but fails to apply himself/herself.

The Phantom Genius - This student's parents think he/she is extremely bright. In reality, this student is an "average" learner under a great deal of pressure to perform.

The Sex Symbol - This student is very attractive and distracts other class members by his/her sheer movements in the classroom.

The Whiner - This student constantly complains about everything from homework to the classroom temperature.

The Operator - This student aims to please and constantly insists on aiding the teacher in some way to gain favor.

The Transient - This student has one goal--to get out of class to roam the halls.

The Giggler - This student finds anything in the classroom to be funny. Usually one giggler leads to several.

The Time Server - This student is just abiding time until the legal age for dropping out.

The Cliffhanger - This student maintains a D- average and only decides to show an academic interest when the grading period is near an end.

The Love Connection - These two students are into writing notes, staring at each other, and holding hands.

The Social Freak - This student loves to talk and plan his/her social calendar.

The Bully - This student tries to display power through cruel statements, threats, and/or displays of temper.

The Drill Sergeant - This student is a master in repeating directions, ordering students around in the classroom, and controling situations.

The California Dreamer - This student tunes out the teacher to explore thoughts of his/her own.

The Mind Game Player - This student's goal is to make the teacher uncomfortable. He/she sits in the classroom, stares, and smiles. No one really knows what he/she is thinking.

Organizing for Group Activities

Cooperative learning is an important teaching methods to incorporate into the classroom. However, some teachers refuse or limit its use due to increased student movement and noise level. Too often, teachers just instruct students to "get into groups of four or five" and then wonder why their group activities are nonproductive. Properly planning for and managing cooperative groups lead to a positive learning experience for students. Some facts related to grouping students are:

1. Cooperative learning promotes positive well being, academic achievement, and positive attitudes, maximizes productivity, and motivates students.

2. Group size (2-5 students) is determined by the type of activity.

3. Teachers should offer individual, paired, and group choices sometimes.

4. There should be a planned method for students to move into their groups.
    a. location
    b. posting
    c. permanent seating (tables, 4 desks together, etc.)

5. Group size should be limited to no more than 5 students per group.

6. Each student should be assigned to a group and a responsibility based on his/her personal needs and abilities. Consider the sex and race of group members. For example, you do not want all girls in one group. *Avoid having students select their own groups.* Individual roles within a group might include:
    a. Leader
    b. Recorder
    c. Reporter
    d. Runner

In the classroom should be posted specific duties of each group member. For example, some typical duties might include:

LEADER
1. *Keep all group members on task*
2. *Keep noise levels low*
3. *Summarize periodically for the group*
4. *Reach group consensus*
5. *Encourage participation by involving members in the group discussion*

RECORDER
1. *Take notes*
2. *Participate in the group discussion*
3. *Outline group decisions*
4. *Prepare the final written report*

REPORTER
1. *Participate in the group discussion*
2. *Take notes of main points*
3. *Prepare oral presentation*
4. *Present the oral report to the class*

RUNNER
1. *Get supplies*
2. *Ask questions for the group and report back any findings*
3. *Participate in the group discussion*
4. *Assist the reporter during the presentation if any visuals or tangibles are used*

7. A group assignment sheet with clear and specific instructions should be used. The purpose should be stated, the steps to completion should be listed, and the expectations or evalution for the final product included. See Example 3-A.

8. Teachers should monitor the activities of each group and provide constructive feedback.

9. Students and teachers should enforce the yard rule during management, and only allow the runner to ask questions of the teacher or raise his/her hand for assistance. Expect the noise level of the class to be higher.

10. Assign individual and group grades. See Examples 3-B, 3-C, 3-D, and 3-E.

Example 3 - A
Group Assignment Sheet

Problem: New Uses for Old Things

Criteria: The new use must be realistic and practical without modification to
the object.

Steps:
1. In each group appoint a leader, recorder, reporter, and runner.
2. Sign the index card at the table designating each person's responsibility.
3. The runner will retrieve a bag from the storage box. The group leader will open the bag.
4. The group will identify the object and list at least 5 current uses for the object. Each use must be different.
5. The group will decide on 3 non-traditional uses for the object. Other items may be used in the development of the new purpose and use.
6. The reporter will present a 3-5 minute demonstration highlighting the traditional uses of the object and them demonstrating one of the new uses for the object.
7. The group will submit a written outline of 5 traditional uses and 3 new uses for the object.

Evaluation: Group participation
Oral group report
Written report

Example 3 - B

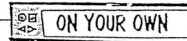

OBSERVATION CHECKLIST

Teacher: _____   Class: _____   Date: _____

Target Skills: _____

Ratings:
+ = Frequently
✓ = Sometimes
O = Not Yet

NAMES OF STUDENTS						COMMENTS
1.						
2.						
3.						
4.						
5.						
6.						
7.						
8.						
9.						
10.						
11.						
12.						
13.						
14.						
15.						
16.						
17.						
18.						
19.						

Example 3-C

INDIVIDUAL OBSERVATION CHECKLIST

Student: _____ Class: _____ Date: _____

Type of Assignment: _____

☐ Teacher Date _____ Signed _____

☐ Peer Date _____ Signed _____

☐ Self Date _____ Signed _____

	Frequently	Sometimes	Not Yet
_____			
• _____	____	____	____
• _____	____	____	____
• _____	____	____	____
• _____	____	____	____
_____			
• _____	____	____	____
• _____	____	____	____
• _____	____	____	____
• _____	____	____	____
_____			
• _____	____	____	____
• _____	____	____	____
• _____	____	____	____
• _____	____	____	____
_____			
• _____	____	____	____
• _____	____	____	____
• _____	____	____	____
• _____	____	____	____

COMMENTS: _____

_____

_____

Example 3 - D

Group: _____

    In the blanks to the left, write the names of all group members including yourself. Then, under each of the 5 criteria, rate yourself and other group members by placing a "1" if that group member met the criteria or a "0" if the student failed to meet minimum expectations. These rating are anonymous, and no class member will see these forms. REMEMBER, SOON YOU WILL BE A TEACHER AND ONE OF YOUR RESPONSIBILITIES WILL BE TO EVALUATE STUDENTS IN AN OBJECTIVE MANNER THAT WILL BE FAIR TO ALL PARTICIPANTS.

NAME	Cooperation	Contributions	Attendance	Reliability	Attitude	TOTAL (5 Points)

Example 3-E
Group/Individual Grade

Student: _____   Group: _____

Activity: _____

    Content (15 points)   _____

    Creativity (10 points)   _____

    Oral Presentation (15 points)   _____

    Visuals (15 points)   _____

    Written Report (15 points)   _____

    Team Participation (15 points)   _____

    Inividual Participation in the
          group (15 points)   _____

                      TOTAL   _____

Group/Individual Grade

Student: _____   Group: _____

Activity: _____

    Content (15 points)   _____

    Creativity (10 points)   _____

    Oral Presentation (15 points)   _____

    Visuals (15 points)   _____

    Written Report (15 points)   _____

    Team Participation (15 points)   _____

    Inividual Participation in the
          group (15 points)   _____

                      TOTAL   _____

Activity 3-C
When Should I use group work?

Instructions: Sometimes teachers do not like group work and complain of the lost time and noise factor. Cooperative learning is an instructional strategy that requires planning, organization, and specific types of assignments. Examine each of the following situations and write *YES* in the blank if the assignment is suitable for group activity; write *NO* in the blank if the assignment would best be achieved through another method. Be ready to justify your answer.

_____ 1. Answering comprehension type questions at the end of a chapter.

_____ 2. Problem solving to find a solution to the social problem of teenage pregnancy.

_____ 3. Practicing math problems.

_____ 4. Copying definitions to vocabulary words.

_____ 5. Rewriting the conclusion to a story.

_____ 6. Drawing a winter scene

_____ 7. Setting up a budget for a household.

_____ 8. Writing a thank you note.

_____ 9. Selecting the best poem written by classmates.

_____10. Inventing a new household item.

Conducting a Group Activity

In order to effectively and efficiently utilize cooperative learning in the classroom, the following steps should be followed:

1. Post names of group members and duties on the blackboard or overhead.
2. If the group assignment is short (1 or 2 steps), write the steps on the board before class. If the assignment is detailed, develop a group assignment sheet (See Example 3 - A).
3. Arrange desks prior to class if possible. On each group area, place a number or color indicator, a notecard, and an assignment sheet (if used).
4. Before class on the board write:
   a. Enter the classroom quietly.
   b. Check for your group number (color) and go to that group area.
   c. Store bookbags, etc. out of the aisles.
   d. Sign the notecard on the desk top.
   e. Sit quietly and wait for further instructions.
5. When ready to begin the activity, remind students of group member duties.
6. Call attention to the purpose of the assignment and the steps to be followed. Read each item from the assignment sheet and question students about what they are to be doing.
7. Clearly state expectations and method(s) of evaluation.
8. Question students again with specifics about the assignment and set time limits.
9. Monitor each group. Pick up signed notecards (this is your attendace).
10. Have students remain in group seating during follow up discussions.

Activity 3-D

Instructions: Examine the following scenario. Using Example 3-A as the assigned activity, explain how you would plan for the groups, post assignments, explain the activity, and assess the groups with minimal noise levels.

Ms. Uno is not pleased with the way that her group activities are progressing. She had hoped that she could complete some administrative duties while students engaged in a meaningful group activity. Although she feels that the assignments are meaningful, that she gives good instructions prior to the activity, and that she allows enough time for work to be completed, some students do not follow directions and many do not finish their work. A few groups finish early and some groups never finish at all. Soon, many of the students are visiting or using free time activities. Ms. Uno has to interrupt her work at her desk to discipline rowdy students or to answer questions. What can she do to improve her situation?

REFLECTION

1. What are some things you like about cooperative learning? Dislike?

2. When should group work be used in the classroom?

3. What are the advantages of group work as compared to lecture and questioning?

4. When is group work inappropriate?

5. What are some management problems you have experienced and/or foresee in using group work?

6. What are some things that teachers can do to ensure success in managing group activities?

Managing Learning Centers

A learning center is any part of the classroom designated for independent, paired, or group learning. The purpose of a learning center is:
1. To provide an alternative to seat work
2. To reward students
3. To provide practice
4. To provide enrichment
5. To encourage cooperation or independence
6. To address individual learner preferences

Learning centers incorporate listening, reading, writing, and speaking within activities which are usually in game or manipulative form. Added pluses are better relationships, collaborative learning, and improved self esteem. Well managed learning centers reduce student conflict in the classroom since students are actively involved with activities that focus on their interests.

When creating a learning center, first select a subject area, and then determine the skill or concept to be taught, reinforced, or enriched. The location of the center and the size of the area in the classroom should be determined since this foreshadows the type of learning center and activities that could be used. Finally, develop the learning center activities and select needed materials and furniture.

In setting up the center, consider the following guidelines:
1. Use dividers and/or furniture to separate centers
2. Create quiet and active centers grouping the types together
3. Provide for individual, paired, and group activities at different centers that are all student centered
4. Mark all materials for the center and specify their storage areas
5. Develop a schedule or rotation system for center use
6. Provide clean up supplies

When teachers introduce centers, they should explain center rules, rotation systems, etc. The activity at each center should be demonstrated for students.

Students should be instructed in where to get and to store supplies and how to record their activities and times at the centers.

New teachers need to remember that learning centers require flexibility on the part of the teacher. The role of the teacher is preparer, introducer, encourager, and manager. Each center is dependent on the teacher to keep it alive and functioning. The teacher is responsible for preparing all the learning tools, updating centers, collecting center resources, and assessing student progress. In managing the centers, teachers should begin with one or two and add to that number as their management skills improve. Also, students at a center should be required to turn in a "product" to demonstrate progress at the center. A successful component of learning centers is student selection. Although teachers should monitor the centers a student visits, students should be given freedom to visit centers of personal choice with appropriate documentation of time and learning accomplishments.

Types of Learning Centers

Although the number and types of learning centers are as limitless as the

imagination, the following are examples of learning centers.

Block Corner

Dramatic Play

*Art

Sand and Water

*Writing

*Library/Magazine Display

*Manipulatives/Math

*Science/Discovery

*Music/Listening

*Logic Center

*Discussion

*Display

*Quiet Zone

*Grooming Center

*Writing Wall/Graffiti Desk

*Appropriate for junior high and secondary classrooms as well as elementary.

Activity 3 - E

Instructions: Select a type of learning center appropriate to your grade or subject area. Return to the diagram of your classroom. Place your learning center in the room. Justify your answer. What materials will you need for your center? What will be your rotation method? How will you maintain accountability for each student's time and learning?

REFLECTIONS

1. Are learning centers appropriate for your classroom. If yes, which ones and why? If no, why not? How could you modify a learning center to meet the needs of your students?

2. List at least 10 places where you can obtain free and/or inexpensive learning center materials.

Quick Tip
Organizing Material

BOOKS

1. Organize by author, theme, or subject.
2. Feature an author each month. Create a bulletin board and provide several of his/her works for students to check-out.
3. Group and label reference materials.
4. Keep a variety of genres.
5. Use colored tape to color code books by genre, author, etc.
6. Group multiple book copies in one place.
7. Use a wooden clothes dryer (v-shaped) or clothes hangers to display magazines.

WRITING

1. Display multiple samples of writing for various assignments. Laminate them in colored folders for easy storage.
2. Store writing materials (paper, pens, etc.) in a designated place that is easily accessible to students.
3. Provide a stapler, paper clips, etc. for students.
4. Have several clipboards near the writing materials for an easy make-shift desk for pair-share or editing activities.

DAILY REQUIREMENTS

1. Have a special place to post daily objectives.
2. Develop an assignment center with daily assignments for every class for a full week.
3. Decorate an "Access to Excess" box for storing folders labeled for each day and containing homework assignments, daily lesson plans and handout sheets. These are for absent students to determine make up work.
4. Create a mailbox center for students to exchange notes/messages and for easy distribution of graded papers.

MATH/SCIENCE

1. Provide an area with extra graphing paper, pencils, rulers, laboratory equipment, etc. Any extra textbooks can be placed here for students who forget their books

Quick Tip
Hang it on the Wall

Functional bulletin boards
Bell/daily schedule
Monthly calendar
Maps
Fire exit (safety) maps
Samples of writing, paper headings, etc.
Athletic schedule
Student announcements from the office
Classroom rules, rewards, and consequences
Current events/school news
Assignment due dates
Cooperative learning roles and duties

Quick Tip
Giving Direction

Giving effective directions for independent practice is essential to a lesson. Consider the following:

1. Only speak when students are quiet.

2. Watch their body language for feedback.

3. Have students put down pencils/pens.

4. If there are more than 2 steps to the assignment, use activity sheets or write them on the board.

5. Do not pass out worksheets or give page numbers until after making the assignment.

6. MODEL! MODEL! Use the guided practice session as means to demonstrate instructions.

7. Post page numbers and question numbers on the board.

8. Ask specific questions of students regarding the directions (What is the first thing you are to do, John?).   Clarify.

9. Monitor closely for compliance.

10. DO NOT go to your desk and sit.

Quick Tip
Types of Groups

1. **Round Robin** - All team members are actively involved in an activity. The teacher gives an assignment and all team members begin to work individually. When time is called, the teacher instructs the students to exchange papers within a group. During the second time interval, students edit the work of their peers and add to the assignment. At the end of a second time interval, the teacher instructs students to exchange papers again. This procedure continues until each student has his/her original paper with corrections and additions.

2. **Partner Check** - Each student works alone to find a solution to a problem and then has an assigned partner to check his/her work or to discuss the solution.

3. **Pairs Check** - This grouping is used with the "partner check" method. After checking for consensus with their partners, students then work with a second pair of students to reach consensus among all four.

4. **Jigsaw** - Each team member has to prepare to teach other members of the group one segment of information or do one piece of the work. Students can jigsaw within their own team or meet with members from other teams with the same assignment.

5. **Numbered Heads Together** - Students in a group are given a number from 1-5. After the teacher asks a question, the group members discuss the answer. The teacher then calls on one of the numbers 1-5 to respond. Only the students with that number can respond to the question.

6. **Cooperative Classroom Teams** - Students are paired and are given the responsibility to look out for their partners. They are responsible for recording assignments for absent partners, assisting each other in class activities, and checking to see that partners complete assignments. If a student has a question, he/she must ask the partner first before inquiring of the teacher.

7. **Group Investigation** - Students are assigned a topic for study and then pursue in-depth investigations of the topic. Each group prepares and presents a written and oral report.

Quick Tip
Group Consideration Summary

The following outline will summarize the role of the teacher, the types of activities suitable for group work, and the decisions related to grouping students.

I. **Role of the Teacher**
   A. **Organizer**
   B. **Facilitator**
   C. **Evaluator**

II. **Types of Activities Suitable to Group Work**
   A. **Problem Solving**
   B. **Research Projects**
   C. **Games**
   D. **Review**
   E. **Brainstorming**
   F. **Tutoring**
   G. **Planning**
   H. **Discussion**

III. **Decisions Related to Grouping**
   A. **Assignment**
   B. **Group Size**
   C. **Room Arrangement**
   D. **Instructional Materials**
   E. **Student Placement**
   F. **Student Responsibilities**

Chapter 4
Classroom Routines (Procedures)

FOCUS

1. To contrast rules and routines (procedures).
2. To identify necessary classroom routines for effective and efficient instruction.
3. To identify the steps necessary in teaching routines.

Routines and Rules

Potentially disruptive problems can be avoided by implementing planned classroom routines or procedures. Routines are designed to maximize instructional classroom time and to assist in daily organization. Just telling a student about a routine is never enough; therefore, the first 2-3 days of school will be spent teaching routines to students. Before actually developing particular routines for the classroom, it is necessary to first differentiate between a classroom rule and a routine.

What is a classroom routine or procedure? Classroom routines or procedures are the way things are done. They answer such questions as what should I do when I enter the classroom? What should I do if I need a question answered? How do I turn in my homework?

How do classroom routines differ from classroom rules? Classroom rules are designed to discipline students in how they behave. When a student breaks a classroom rule, there are penalties involved. With classroom routines, there are no penalties. The routine is retaught.

How do students learn classroom routines or procedures?
When teaching a classroom routine, the teacher first defines and demonstrates the routine to the class. Students are then allowed to rehearse the routine. The teacher must remember that students are not punished for failing to follow a routine. Instead, they are retaught. Finally, the routine is continually reinforced through evaluation and reteaching over the school year.

Reflection

1. Your classroom will be your new home for the next 9 months. In order to live in harmony with others, you have established certain routines or ways of handling everyday occurrences in your personal life. Identify 2 routines that occur in your home daily.

2. You must establish routines to ensure efficient and effective instruction in the classroom. Think back on your classroom experiences as a student, observer and/or teacher. Identify 3 noises that bothered you most. Identify 3 which bothered you the least.

       most bothersome   *least bothersome*

3. Identify 3 student movements which bother you?

4. List 5 administrative duties and/or daily occurrences that may prevent your classroom from running efficiently and effectively. (Example: sharpening pencils).

ACTIVITY 4 - A
DEVELOPING CLASSROOM ROUTINES

Instructions: Consider each of the following situations. Determine first if you consider the item a routine, a behavior that should be addressed by a classroom rule (consider the differences between the two), or ignored. If the item should be handled by a rule, write "rule" in the blank space; if you feel the item should neither be addressed as a routine or a rule, write "none" in the space; for each routine, decide on at least 3 different ways to handle the situation through a routine. Some routine can accomplish two or more activities.

1. returning papers

2. collecting papers

3. filing student papers

4. entering the classroom

5. tardy admissions

6. **bathroom privileges**

7. **water privileges**

8. **note passing**

9. **throwing away trash**

10. **sharpening pencils**

11. **stopping the classroom buzz**

12. starting class

13. dismissing class

14. enrichment activities

15. calling roll

16. collecting money

17. leaving the room as a group

18. paper headings

19. seating

20. no pencil

21. no paper

22. no textbook

23. student movement during class such as tapping a pencil

24. evacuations

25. returning signed papers from parents

26. reviewing corrected tests

27. free time

28. checking homework

29. make-up assignments

30. **permission to speak**

31. **students seeking help from the teacher**

32. **putting away coats, books, etc.**

33. **movement into groups**

34. **eating in class**

35. **drinking in class**

36. gum chewing

37. calling on students to answer
    questions, etc.

38. students reading out loud in
    class

39. students reading silently

40. make up test

41. cheating

42. giving out rewards or
    detentions

43. keeping students after school
    or during class

44. mass punishment

45. field trips

46. students refusing to
    participate

47. failure to buy school supplies
    or pay fees

48. failure to pay fees for field
    trip or return permission slips

49. students not attending special
    assemblies

50. using the telephone

51. students who run out of
    materials

52. students who want to visit the
    counselor, coach, etc.

53. a child who is sick

54. **students who finish early**

55. **violence occurs in the classroom**

56. **students who just walk out**

57. **students who destroy materials**

58. **assigning responsibilities**

59. **cleaning the classroom**

60. reminders for long term
    assignments

61. contacting parents

62. determining excused and
    unexcused absences

63. students taking medication

64. tattlers

65. allowing students to use your
    personal resources

66. _____

67. _____

Activity 4 -B

Instructions: Select one of the routines that you have described and write a script explaining the routine to a class.

Chapter 5
Why Do Students Misbehave?

Focus

1. To list basic needs of students.
2. To identify mistaken goals of students.
3. To assess the roles of preventive, supportive, and corrective discipline in classroom management.

Student Needs

According to Rudolf Dreikurs, by nature students are social creatures who want to belong and who choose to behave or misbehave to fill a personal need. All children need to feel that they can achieve something, to know that others care about them, to realize that they can influence others, to recognize the importance of giving freely, and to enjoy life. William Glasser (1993) founded his Control Theory on two important principles: First, behavior is related to intrinsic needs, and secondly all human behavior, appropriate or inappropriate, is an attempt to satisfy those personal needs. He identifies this hierarchy of needs as:

> Fun
>
> Freedom
>
> Power
>
> Love/Belonging
>
> Survivial

For example, a student has an intrinsic need to have power. To satisfy this need, a student might take a positive approach and become a member of student senate or a club officer. Just as easily, this same student may choose to become the school bully or join a violent gang to get the attention or recognition he/she desires.

REFLECTION

1. Define each of these needs.

    Survival

    Belonging

    Power

    Fun

    Freedom

Activity 5 - A

Instructions: Complete the following outline by identifying ways that basic needs are unfilled in Column B and listing ways teachers/schools might satisfy the basic needs of students in Column C.

Column A Basic Need	Column B Ways Unfulfilled	Column C Ways to Fulfill
Survival		
Belonging/Love		
Power/Control		
Freedom		
Fun		

Mistaken Goals

In his works, Rudolf Dreikurs identified 4 categories of inappropriate behavior or "mistaken goals" which students utilize when personal needs are not being met. They include:

Attention Getting
Power Seeking
Revenge Seeking
Displaying Inadequacy

ATTENTION GETTING can be associated with the basic needs of survival and belonging. Whether the attention is positive or negative, the individual is driven by the force for someone to notice him/her. Examples of attention getting behaviors are students acting as the class clown, excessive talking, tugging at the teacher's clothing, running in the classroom, and forgetting materials.

If a student feels that the teacher has not responded to his/her attention getting tactics, he/she may seek *POWER*. With this mistaken goal, the student challenges the teacher with comments such as "Come make me," "Don't touch me," and "There's a law against that." The student may show signs of hostility, aggression, disobedience, or stubbornness.

If a student feels that a teacher or school district is not responding to his/her goals of attention and power, the student may seek REVENGE by being rude, hurtful, or destructive. This student may act out his/her mistaken goal(s) through such actions as name calling, destroying a teacher's personal belongings, stealing from the teacher, or threatening the teacher.

Sometimes, students tend to totally withdraw from school and identify with the mistaken goal of *inadequacy*. In this situation, the student feels there is no hope for his/her success and that no one really cares or understands. He/she will sleep in class, fail to do homework, refuse to participate in discussions or activities, quit tasks easily, fail to attend school, or use forms of escape such as drugs.

How does a teacher determine the mistaken goal of a student? First, the teacher needs to identify the problem and to determine what the unsatisfied need of the student is to prevent the possibility of reinforcing inappropriate behavior. For example, a student who constantly talks during class needs attention. When the teacher constantly reprimands the student in front of peers to get quiet, the teacher is providing the attention the student desires. Therefore, the misbehavior will likely continue. However, if the teacher first recognizes the problem and identifies the need of the student, then positive recognition to satisfy the student's need can be given such as greeting the student each day, calling on the student to answer in class, or assigning the person the task of group reporter during cooperative learning.

A second methods to indicate the type of mistaken goal is for the teacher to examine his/her feelings toward the student after the behavior. The following chart taken from C. M. Charles (1996) outlines the mistaken goal and the teacher's feeling:

MISTAKEN GOAL	TEACHER'S FEELING
Attention	Annoyed
Power	Angry
Revenge	Hurt
Inadequacy	Helpless

Another method is to identify mistaken goals is for the teacher to observe the student's behavior after correction. C. M. Charles (1996) lists the following examples:

If the student:	*then the goal is:*
stops the behavior and then repeats it	Attention
refuses to stop or increases misbehavior	Power
becomes violent or hostile	Revenge
refuses to cooperate, participate, or interact	Inadequacy

In summary, when faced with the problem of determining the true motive behind misbehavior, the teacher should ask questions such as:

What is the problem?
What is the student's real need?
What is the mistaken goal of the student?
How can I avoid reinforcing the mistaken goal?
What can I do to fulfill the student's need in this class.

Once the true need of the student has been identified, the teacher should confront the student with the negative behavior and discuss the true motive behind the action. A sincere effort should be made by the teacher to find out how he/she can help the student in a positive way.

Discipline

In the classroom, a teacher's goal is to provide a classroom environment that is stable, safe, and conducive to learning. Unfortunately, some students infringe on the rights of the teacher and other students. When this occurs, it is the duty of the teacher to discipline students for their inappropriate behaviors. Discipline is not to be confused with punishment. The following chart contrasts punishment and discipline:

PUNISHMENT	DISCIPLINE
Stresses teacher authority	Based on logical consequences
Consist of retribution/revenge	Concerned with changing behavior
Punisher assumes responsibility correcting behavior	Student is responsible for correcting behavior
Closes options for students	Keeps options open for modification
Negative and short term	Personal and long term
Expresses anger/disappointment	Expresses concern
Expedient	Challenging

C. M. Charles (1996) refers to discipline as having three faces: preventive, corrective, and supportive discipline. Preventive discipline creates a learning environment that prevents misbehavior; supportive discipline recognizes and assists students at the first indications of misbehavior; and corrective discipline suppresses and redirects misbehavior in a positive way.

Preventive and Supportive Discipline

No technique related to preventive discipline is more effective than good planning. Teachers who are prepared, who clearly state their behavior expectations, who plan motivating student centered lessons of high interest, and who implement the lesson with enthusiasm and confidence experience minimal discipline problems. At times, some teachers rationalize their failure to properly plan lessons with the fact that "no one else does it that detailed" or "that takes up too much time." Perhaps this is when teachers need to decide if they prefer to spend their time planning or disciplining students?

> Areas to consider in preventing problems before they occur include:
> 1. Developing student self-esteem.
> 2. Empowering students with classroom decisions.
> 3. Providing clear instructions (say it, model it, question students, and repeat)
> 4. Relating content to the real world and student needs
> 5. Modeling courtesy and good manners.
> 6. Developing an open, positive classroom environment.
> 7. Including parents in the management process
> 8. Beginning the school year with established routines for students.

An important part of preventive and supportive discipline is the teacher's ability to manage large groups, subgroups, and individuals. Jacob Kounin coined the term "withitness" to describe teachers who know what is going on in the class at all times. According to Kounin, desisting the right student(s) is essential in sending the students a message that "I see what is going on and who is doing it." Blaming the wrong student or removing the "victim" of the misbehavior only sends a message that the teacher is not truly aware of the misbehavior instigator. A second key to withitness is timing--knowing when to stop inappropriate behavior before it spreads throughout the classroom. Attending to possible problems before they escalate promotes a more efficient and effective classroom.

Kounin, also, describes the "ripple effect" which may occur positively or negatively. For example, if three students in the class are behaving appropriately, the teacher recognizes these students, and the other children immediately try to model the appropriate behavior. In the negative sense, a teacher reprimands students for their misbehavior, and students around them start demonstrating appropriate behavior. It should be noted that this "ripple effect" is more successful with young elementary children, and its effectiveness diminishes over the school year.

Other methods that Kounin describes that address preventive and supportive discipline are overlapping, movement management, group focus, and satiation. Overlapping is attending to more than one issue at a time. It includes working with individuals during independent practice and at the same time monitoring the whole class for on-task behavior. Movement management relates to the lesson and describes the lesson's pacing and transitions. Wasting time between activities, losing time to get necessary materials from a cabinet, and stopping to write lengthy notes on a blackboard are all examples of poor movement management. According to Kounin, materials necessary for the lesson must be readily available, teaching equipment must be set up and in working condition, and the teacher should use whatever technique ensures efficient and effective instruction. During group focus, preventive discipline stresses student attention. The teacher can best achieve this by calling on students at random and avoiding predictable patterns. Teachers who hold the attention of every member throughout a lesson are more successful in student involvement.

In order to prevent student boredom with a subject, teachers need to be aware of satiation or giving too much information or practice once students have mastered the concept. Challenging activities and varied teacher methods stimulate students in learning. Why require students to complete 25 sentences or problems when it is clear that the students understand the concept? Teachers should constantly scan the classroom making eye contact with students to determine their lesson interest and to prevent lesson satiation.

Haim Ginott approaches preventive and supportive discipline in recognizing the importance of the social-emotional atmosphere in the classroom. He emphasized that students are people, too, and that teachers have greater impact when they respect students and serve as personal role models. The use of "sane messages," in which the teacher merely describes the issue or event of concern. leaves the student's self-esteem intact and allows students to examine situations and develop their own solutions in a non-judgmental environment.

Fredric Jones examined classroom misbehavior and noted the following:

1. 50% of instructional time is lost because students are off-task.
2. There are 2 types of common misbehavior: talking (80%) and goofing off (20%).
3. Misbehaviors occur most often during independent practice.

Jones felt that lost teaching time could be salvaged if three things were implemented by teachers--effective body language, incentive systems, and efficient individual help.

Body language includes eye contact, physical proximity, body carriage, facial expression, and gestures. Every teacher should develop a "teacher look" in which students readily recognize ENOUGH. First year teachers should practice this teacher look in front of a mirror and be ready for its introduction into the classroom. Sometimes teachers are described as having "the walk and talk" or "being a natural." This means that the teacher physically carries himself/herself in a confident and respectful manner, and that he/she feels in control of the situation. Students read a teacher's body language and recognize if the teacher feels in control or intimidated. The proper use of facial expressions and hand gestures prevent the teacher from ever having to break the flow of a lesson. A mere palm out or shake of the head identifies disapproval for student behavior. Proximity is important in body language, particularly at the junior high and high school levels. Adolescents like their space. When a teacher moves into that space, the student usually discontinues the misbehavior and pulls away. For example if two students are talking, the teacher should walk and stand between them. The lesson has not stopped, but generally the talking ceases. Sometimes placing a hand on the desktop or the back of a student's desk quickly sends a message to a student that the teacher recognizes the misbehavior and wants it to stop immediately.

Incentives fall under three categories--genuine, grandma rule, and educational value. Genuine incentives are those things seen as important to students such as free time, watching a movie in class, or having class outside. The grandma rule is simple--let's do this first and then I have a treat for you. Students are not given the reward unless the appropriate action occurs. Things of educational value include an educational activity that students enjoy doing such as physical education, art or music for elementary students and choices in topics, watching a movie about a novel just completed, or library time for junior high and high school students.

An area of concern for some teachers is during independent practice when students are seeking help in completing assignments while doing individual work at their desks. When a teacher spends too much time with one student, others feel hopelessly lost and unable to continue the assignment. What happens? They flap their arms in the air, make comments to neighbors, and sometimes are totally off task, they talk, make noises, write notes, etc.

In order to prevent this problem, Jones recommends arranging the room in a "U" shape so that students are easily accessible and limiting time to no more than 20 seconds per student. Jones suggests that teachers comment on the work completed, hint or suggest the next step, and leave. To prevent hands flapping in the air, the teacher should develop a routine using color coded signs of red and green to indicate whether the student needs help.

Preventive and supportive discipline requires that a teacher not sit at a desk or position himself/herself at the front of the room on a stool behind a podium. Instead, the teacher should be actively involved in monitoring behavior and instruction.

Activity 5 - B

Instructions: Review each of the preventive and supportive discipline strategies and determine appropriate grade levels and the advantages and disadvantages of each type.

Strategy	Definition	Appropriate Grade Level	Advantages	Disadvantages

****

Withitness

Ripple Effect

Overlapping

Movement Mgt.

Group Focus

Satiation

Sane Messages

Body Language

Proximity

Incentives

Efficient Help

Corrective Discipline

Most students want to behave and gain teacher approval. That is why preventive and supportive discipline are effective in handling some inappropriate student behaviors. However, when students break school rules, corrective discipline is necessary. In such cases, teachers should immediately stop the inappropriate behavior, invoke a logical consequence, and follow-up with the student to make certain that the inappropriate behavior has ceased. Below is a brief description of several discipline theories appropriate for corrective discipline.

1. Fritz Redyl and William Wattenberg stressed the importance of identifying student motives for misbehavior because only through their identification could misbehavior be corrected. Within their theory, however, they stressed the importance of student empowerment and emotional health. While most will agree with this theory, few teachers have the time to implement it fully.

2. Skinner's behavior modification theory is effective in changing behavior. His ideas include "Catch 'Em Being Good," token economies, praise, rewards, and contracts for appropriate behavior. Behavior modification works and if implemented systematically, it works well. However, questions arise as to whether or not rewards promote or hinder intrinsic motivation for appropriate behavior. Some view Skinner's theory as mind control and bribery while others see it as a workable system in which students feel successful. Unfortunately for some teachers, behavior modification is not considered to be an effective corrective discipline technique for all students since it is cumbersome, slow, time consuming and financially difficult.

3. Lee Canter's Assertive Discipline Plan is used in many school systems. It is based on rules that are consistently enforced with appropriate consequences and positive rewards. It is considered to be "fair," and teachers feel it provides corrective discipline through its consequences. Some critics of the model, however, are concerned that Assertive Discipline is too aggressive and harsh and that the focus is on suppressing inappropriate behavior and not instilling appropriate behavior.

4. William Glasser stresses that students freely make choices and must live with those choices. His theory is not related to the conditions of their past but to the present situation.

Glasser stresses that if needs are met, students will respond positively. His "accept no excuses" promotes the idea that students must confront the consequences for their behaviors and can not blame their actions on external events. He emphasizes the importance of well planned and exciting classes that stimulate students in a safe, academic school environment. Teachers are considered to be lead manager--that is a management technique in which the teacher and student work together to discover the real nature of the misbehavior and mutually examine the problem and agree on a solution. Of the corrective discipline models discussed, Glasser's reality therapy offers students the opportunity to become self-directed and responsible for controlling their behavior.

Reflection

1. Of the four corrective methods described, which do you feel to be the most appropriate for the grade level you plan to teach? Why?

2. Which corrective models could be combined in developing a discipline plan?

Quick Tip
Common Misbehaviors

Behavior	Child's Purpose	Common Reaction	Helpful Reaction
Show Off	To be noticed by doing something shocking	Notice and react to the behavior	Ignore the behavior and remove the child from the situation
Push to the Limit	To push as far possible and then stop before getting into serious trouble	Give continuos warnings or start to count-down	Give no warning and immediately apply a consequence
Gives Up Easily	To get as much as possible with little effort	Tell children to try harder	Break up task into smaller assignments and reward after the completion of a task
The Quiz Kid	To keep the adult busy by asking questions	Answer questions	Answer a question with a question
Bedevil-ment	To keep adults on edge by playing tricks	Warn child to stop	Say nothing and apply a consequence
Busy Bee	To appear to be working very hard	Allow for extra time	Set limits and follow through
Chatterbox	To gain recognition through tattling, cute sayings, etc.	Laugh or comment	Ignore the remarks
Goodness	To be noticed and gain approval for being good	Remark how good the child is	Give attention when not expected

Behavior	Child's Purpose	Common Reaction	Helpful Reaction
Laziness	To keep the adult involved while stalling for time	Prod, coax, or threaten	Apply a consequence
Dependent	To get others to do things for them	Do the task for the child	Help the child get started and then allow them to to complete the task
Tired	To get prefer-ential treatment	Help the child	Apply consequences
Shy	To avoid active situations	Excuse them	Provide, short, non-threatening ways for child to express self
Fearful	To prove helpless	Sympathize	Discuss fear and devise a plan to overcome
Self-Indulgent	To get others io do things for him/her	Do things for the child	Allow child to do own task
Charmer	To use person-ality to get attention	Indulge child's needs	Recognize only actual accomplishments
Clinger	To look to adult for support	Encourage behavior because adult feels needed	Spend some time with child and some time away
Good Looks	To get what he/she wants	Overlook misbehavior because child is cute	Recognize only actual accomplishments

Quick Tip
Encouraging Good Behavior

In order to encourage good behavior, a teacher should:

1. be prepared with exciting, student-centered lessons and activities.
2. develop materials that will ensure some degree of success
3. allow choices for students
4. express clear and specific behavior expectations to students
5. incorporate cooperative learning activities in the classroom
6. be the adult
7. avoid arguments, confrontations, and temper fits
8. be human
9. be consistent
10. be fair without treating every student the same
11. promote student self-esteem
12. give students responsibility
13. greet students daily and call on them by name
14. be willing to give time and effort
15. share with students
16. be flexible
17. recognize accomplishments no matter how minimal and openly compliment students
18. create a warm friendly classroom
19. admit personal mistakes
20. model good behavior for students
21. be interested in what they do outside of classroom and attend extra-curricular activities
22. Stop and listen to students

Chapter 6
Classroom Rules, Rewards, and Consequences

School District Discipline Policies

Local school districts have the right to adopt reasonable rules and regulations to govern student conduct to ensure the efficient functioning of the school. As an employee within a school district, it is your responsibility to enforce all school rules. Generally, before a student may be punished, the pupil must be informed as to expectations of conduct through written statement, oral instruction, or observance of general custom. Most school districts accomplish this through a discipline handbook.

ACTIVITY 6 - A

Instructions: Using a discipline handbook from a local school district, examine the school policies and answer the following questions.

1. Does the school district allow corporal punishment? If so, what procedures must be followed?

2. What are some of the possible disciplinary actions for misconduct?

3. Distinguish between suspension and expulsion? What process must be followed in student suspension? expulsion?

4. What procedural guidelines are established for special education students?

5. Identify at least 3 school wide rules that you will be required to enforce.

Classroom Rules

An important part of any classroom management plan is a list of classroom rules. Well managed classrooms take considerable time to establish, but when rules are taught and consequences enforced, time is saved all year long. Remember, all classroom rules must be within the limitations of the district/school discipline policy. Developing appropriate classroom rules is a difficult task. The general principles of good classroom rules include:

- Short term solutions do not solve long term problems.
- Classroom rules must take into consideration the needs of teachers and students.
- Rules should bring about long term change.
- Good classroom discipline programs teach students to impose personal limits.
- Students must be held responsible for their own actions.
- It is humane to discipline children.
- Classroom rules have little if any impact on severe discipline problems.

Two models directly related to classroom rules, consequences, and rewards are Behavior Modification (B. F. Skinner) and Assertive Discipline (Lee Canter). According to Skinner, behavior is shaped by consequences, and a systematic use of rewards can shape that student's behavior positively. Two important principles of behavior modification are appropriate behavior should be rewarded and inappropriate behavior ignored. Canter's Assertive Discipline model has 4 key points:

- Teachers have a right to establish a classroom structure that provides for an optimal learning environment.
- Teachers have a right to determine and request appropriate behavior to meet the teacher's need.
- Teachers have a right to expect assistance from parents and administrators when disciplining a child.
- Students have a right to make choices but with consequences.

ACTIVITY 6 - B

Instructions: Examine the scenario below. How would Skinner address the problem? Canter?

In a 6th grade class, Bubba was a belligerent child who would constatly confront the teacher's authority by refusing to do his work. Every day it was the same thing. If the teacher mentioned anything to him, he would become hostile and try to start a confrontation.

Skinner   Canter

Activity 6 - C

Instructions: Listed below are several classroom rules taken from posted classroom discipline plans. Indicate if the statement is a general or specific rule by circling "G" for general or "S" for specific. If the wording of the rule could be improved, rewrite it in the space provided.

G   S   1. Do not disturb others from learning.

G   S   2. Raise quiet hands to talk.

G   S   3. No name calling or put downs.

G   S.   4. Come to class with all materials.

G   S   5. Come to class with PMA (positive mental attitude).

G   S   6. No foul language.

G   S   7. Keep hands, feet, and objects to yourself.

G   S   8. Respect others.

G   S   9. Do right!

G   S   10. Complete work on time.

G   S   11. Use all supplies appropriately.

G   S   12. No eating, drinking, or chewing gum in class.

G   S   13. Do not leave the classroom without permission.

G   S   14. No stealing.

G   S   15. Cooperate with others at school.

G   S   16. Work independently.

G   S   17. Come to class on time.

G   S   18. Enter the class quietly.

G   S   19. No fighting.

G   S   20. Do not turn in messy papers.

Classroom rules are developed in one of four ways. First, the teacher may develop all classroom rules. This method allows for no student involvement and is dependent solely on the teacher's idea of a positive learning environment. A second method is teacher made with student approval. In other words, the teacher presents a specific list of classroom rules, discusses their meanings, and allows students to comment. Once agreed upon, students are obligated to follow all rules. A third method is teacher/student developed. In this method, the teacher shares with the class some general principles for the class to run smoothly such as showing respect, being fair, and promoting learning for all students. Students then brainstorm a list of rules based on these principles and either the teacher or the students select the best 3-5 rules for the classroom. A variation of this method is allowing students the opportunity to develop important classroom principles for a safe, productive classroom and then the teacher develops the classroom rules to meet these student needs. A fourth method is to empower students by allowing them the opportunity to make the classroom rules. In this process, students are advised of unacceptable rules such as those that violate school policy, oppose law, violate values, and interfere with the teacher's goals or style of teaching.

In summary, the steps for writing classroom rules are:

1. Determine basic principles you want in the classroom such as property loss and damage, health and safety, an environment free of serious disruptions, and students working toward an educational purpose.

2. Select the best method for developing rules. Beginning teachers may want to develop 2 or 3 rules and have students develop 2 or 3 after classroom principles are discussed. To empower students is important when developing rules and consequences.

3. Write rules that are clearly and positively stated in behavioral form.

4. Limit rules to 5 or less.

Classroom rules should be posted in the classroom with a list of consequences and rewards. They should be readable from all parts of the classroom. It is the teacher's responsibility to teach the rules to students and to enforce consequences associated with the rules. If at any time a rule no longer is suitable to a class, the teacher can omit it and add a more appropriate rule. It is important to remember that rules are not the only thing to consider when developing a management plan. Unfortunately, some new teachers enter the classroom armed with a poster of words and believe that they will have no discipline problems. Remember that planning and routines are essential to good management. There are no sure fixes when dealing with students.

Activity 6 - D

Instructions: Using the steps outlined on the previous page, develop 3-5 classroom rules appropriate for the grade level/subject you will be teaching.

1. What kind of principles will I want in my classroom?

     a.

     b.

     c.

     d.

     e.

2. Now write 3-5 classroom rules appropriate to the grade level you plan to teach.

     a.

     b.

     c.

     d.

     e.

Consequences and Rewards

Once classroom rules are determined, then appropriate consequences and rewards must be decided. Without question, the teacher should avoid ineffective consequences such as lecturing to students, sarcasm, public apologies, spanking, and sending students out of the room. What then would be an appropriate consequence? Some questions to ask are: Does it work? Does the teacher and student leave with self-esteem in tact? Does the consequence demand responsibility? Does the consequence teach an alternative to the misbehavior? Does the student remain in the classroom?

Consequences for misbehavior should be planned and unpleasant with the ultimate goal of behavior being directed in a positive direction. NEVER SHOULD ACADEMIC WORK BE USED AS A CONSEQUENCE OR PUNISHMENT FOR MISBEHAVIOR. For example, giving students 25 extra math problems for homework because he/she was talking only teaches the student to hate math.

Lee Canter stresses that every teacher should learn to set limits in the classroom. Once rules have been established and discussed in class, the teacher should monitor the class and directly state behavior expectations through hints ("All students should be working individually."); I-messages ("With so much noise, I can't concentrate."); and demands ("Everyone sit down now!"). Limits should be delivered through a combination of voice, eye contact, and gestures. Every teacher needs to develop a "teacher look" that emphatically expresses that the "limit" has been reached.

When students break a rule, use a combination of proximity, eye-contact, and privacy to correct the student. Be as physically close as possible to your students when delivering the consequence. State the broken rule and the consequence. Make eye contact (being aware of cultures that view eye contact as disrespectful), and be sure the only person who hears your message is the student to whom it is directed. Be firm, clear, and committed. Strength at this point comes from knowing that you are doing the right thing. Remember that you want to be "fair" and not necessarily "equal." A meaningful consequence for one student may not impact another. Your goal is for the student to improve his/her behavior and not necessarily to experience a particular consequence. At times it may be appropriate for students to decide on their own consequences for inappropriate behavior. Always control your anger and accept no excuses for inappropriate behavior. Never allow a confrontation to take place in front of a class. Diffuse all power struggles immediately.

Canter states that once teachers have met their limits, they must follow through with planned, logical consequences. Just as the development of classroom rules took time and planning, consequences require the same type of consideration. They should be determined in advance and posted in the classroom. An example of proposed consequences for inappropriate behavior might look like the following:

- Warning (verbal or nonverbal)

- Name written down - 10 minute detention

- Check by name - 20 minute detention

- Second check - Parent/Teacher Conference

- Third check - Conference with disciplinarian

In order for the consequence to be meaningful, it must be reasonable and logical. For example, if a student fails to do homework, it is not logical to give him/her a "0" for the assignment. The logical thing is to have the student complete the homework at recess or lunch.

Just as misbehavior should be monitored and punished, appropriate behavior should be rewarded. There are multiple ways to reward students as individuals and as groups. These might include:

Personal attention such as verbal praise, smiles, and friendly eye contact
Positive notes to parents
Special awards
Special privileges such as class helper
Material rewards that include graphics (charts, stars, posters) and tangible
    items such as stickers, decals, badges, etc.
Home rewards in which parents reward the student with extra TV time,
    special articles of clothing, money, etc.
Group rewards such as watching a special movie with popcorn, no
    homework, a party, class outside, or free time to listen to music.

In summary, consequences for breaking classroom rules should relate to the misbehavior and follow an established sequence. Implementing classroom rules, consequences, and rewards should include the following:

1. Develop classroom rules, consequences, and rewards.

2. Get principal approval.

3. Send a letter home to parents outlining the rules, consequences and rewards, and have parents sign and return a sheet verifying that they have read the information.

4. Post and discuss the rules, consequences, and rewards in the classroom with students.

5. Have students write the rules in their notebooks.

6. Implement the plan immediately.

Activity 6 - E

Instructions: Examine each set of rules, consequences, and rewards below. Using the criteria for good rules, make revisions. For what grade level would each set be appropriate? Select one revised set that you like best. How would your explain the rules, rewards, and consequeces to a class?

Sample I

Rules:
1. Be considerate of others at all times.
2. Do your best work.
3. Use quiet voices in the classroom.
4. Use signals to request permission or to receive help.

Consequences
1. Verbal comments
2. Reports to parents
3. In-class isolation
4. Principal's office

Rewards
1. Positive verbal feedback
2. Tangible rewards
3. Positive reports to parents

Sample II
Rules
1. Bring all materials to class
2. Be attentive while others are talking
3. Bring no food or drink to class.
4. Remain in your seat at the end of the period until the teacher dismisses you
5. Profanity and verbal abuse are not tolerated.

Consequence
1. Warning
2. Call to parents
3. Referral to counselor
4. Referral to detention

Rewards
1. Personal gratification
2. Positive feedback
3. Positive parent calls

Sample III
Rules
1. Come to class on time and be in your seat when the bell rings
2. Bring your book, notebook, and sharpened pencil every day.
3. Work quietly at your seat unless you have permission to do otherwise.
4. Food and drink are not allowed.

Consequences
1. Mark down on citizenship grade

Reward
1. Positive verbal feedback

Sample IV
Rules
1. Pay attention in class.
2. Keep hands and feet to yourself.
3. Do not prevent others from learning.
4. Follow directions and complete assignments.

Consequences
1. Fill out "See Me" card
2. Teacher Conference at lunch. Student will respond in writing to what was I doing? What should I have been doing? What is my plan to improve my behavior?
3. After 3 "See Me" conferences, the student must write or call parents about the misbehavior.
4. Give up coupons for good behavior

Rewards
1. Coupons

Sample V
Rules
1. Treat others as we ourselves would like to be treated.
2. Be on time, prepared to work and stay on task.
3. No eating or drinking in class.

Consequences
1. Two warnings
2. Sit in another teacher's room to complete work
3. Principal's Office

Rewards
1. Verbal praise

Sample VI
Rules
1. Respect others.
2. Raise hands.
3. Work quietly.
4. Be orderly.

Consequences
1. Physical gesture of disapproval
2. Time out - 10 minutes
3. Negative note to parents
4. Stay in at recess or lunch

Rewards
1. Tangible items
2. Positive physical gestures and expression
3. Positive verbal feedback
4. Thank you note to students
5. Positive notes/call to parents

Sample VII

Rules
1. Listen and follow directions
2. Respect and use kind words toward others
3. Keep hands, feet, and other objects to yourself.
4. Complete all assignments on time.
5. Respect school property and the property of others.

Consequences
1. Verbal warning
2. Conference with the teacher
3. After school detention
4. Parent/teacher conference
5. Teacher/Principal conference

Rewards
1. Charts
2. Tokens

Quick Tip
See Me Card

On the following page is a "See Me!" card master duplication sheet. Copy several sheets, back them with cardboard, laminate them, cut them into three cards, and use them as disciplinary referral slips. If a student is misbehaving, simply go to his/her desk and give him/her one of the "See Me!" cards. The detention after class or at lunch can be an oral conversation or a written response followed by a conference.

SEE ME!

During lunch recess TODAY be prepared to discuss the following questions:

What is my goal in this class?

What was I doing in class today?

Was my action helping me to achieve my goal in class?

What is my plan to improve my behavior?

SEE ME!

During lunch recess TODAY be prepared to discuss the following questions:

What is my goal in this class?

What was I doing in class today?

Was my action helping me to achieve my goal in class?

What is my plan to improve my behavior?

SEE ME!

During lunch recess TODAY be prepared to discuss the following questions:

What is my goal in this class?

What was I doing in class today?

Was my action helping me to achieve my goal in class?

What is my plan to improve my behavior?

Quick Tip
Coupons

To reward students for appropriate behavior, use the coupon masters on the next several pages. Xerox copies of the pages, laminate on cardboard, and cut to individual sizes. The Punch Card (Page 140) and the Behavior Card (Page 141) are designed to allow students to credit several appropriate behaviors before a reward. The teacher punches a hole in the card or initials each spot to indicate appropriate behavior. After all slots have been punched or signed, the student exchanges it for a tangible reward. "Hot Shot" (Page 142) cards and "Good Bucks" (Page 143) are used in a token system where cards or bucks are exchanged for rewards. All other coupons are given ONCE a six or 9 weeks period after a student has demonstrated appropriate behavior for the previous grading period.

PUNCH CARD

Earn punches, for PRIZES, for classwork, homework, and good behavior.

Student
Signature_____

PUNCH CARD

Earn punches, for PRIZES, for classwork, homework, and good behavior.

Student
Signature_____

PUNCH CARD

Earn punches, for PRIZES, for classwork, homework, and good behavior.

Student
Signature_____

PUNCH CARD

Earn punches, for PRIZES, for classwork, homework, and good behavior.

Student
Signature_____

PUNCH CARD

Earn punches, for PRIZES, for classwork, homework, and good behavior.

Student
Signature_____

PUNCH CARD

Earn punches, for PRIZES, for classwork, homework, and good behavior.

Student
Signature_____

141

Behavior Credit Card

Name:_____

1 2 3 4 5 6 7 8 9 10

Behavior Credit Card

Name:_____

1 2 3 4 5 6 7 8 9 10

Behavior Credit Card

Name:_____

1 2 3 4 5 6 7 8 9 10

Behavior Credit Card

Name:_____

1 2 3 4 5 6 7 8 9 10

Behavior Credit Card

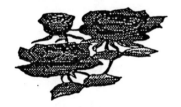

Name:_____

1 2 3 4 5 6 7 8 9 10

Behavior Credit Card

Name:_____

1 2 3 4 5 6 7 8 9 10

Behavior Credit Card

Name:_____

1 2 3 4 5 6 7 8 9 10

Behavior Credit Card

Name:_____

1 2 3 4 5 6 7 8 9 10

CAUGHT YOU!!!

*Collect and save "Hot Shot" cards and redeem
for special rewards.*

CAUGHT YOU!!!

*Collect and save "Hot Shot" cards and redeem
for special rewards.*

CAUGHT YOU!!!

*Collect and save "Hot Shot" cards and redeem
for special rewards.*

CAUGHT YOU!!!

*Collect and save "Hot Shot" cards and redeem
for special rewards.*

CAUGHT YOU!!!

*Collect and save "Hot Shot" cards and redeem
for special rewards.*

CAUGHT YOU!!!

*Collect and save "Hot Shot" cards and redeem
for special rewards.*

CAUGHT YOU!!!

*Collect and save "Hot Shot" cards and redeem
for special rewards.*

CAUGHT YOU!!!

*Collect and save "Hot Shot" cards and redeem
for special rewards.*

CAUGHT YOU!!!

*Collect and save "Hot Shot" cards and redeem
for special rewards.*

CAUGHT YOU!!!

*Collect and save "Hot Shot" cards and redeem
for special rewards.*

CAUGHT YOU!!!

*Collect and save "Hot Shot" cards and redeem
for special rewards.*

CAUGHT YOU!!!

*Collect and save "Hot Shot" cards and redeem
for special rewards.*

CAUGHT YOU!!!

*Collect and save "Hot Shot" cards and redeem
for special rewards.*

CAUGHT YOU!!!

*Collect and save "Hot Shot" cards and redeem
for special rewards.*

COUPON
LIBRARY PASS
Use this coupon to go to the library to read, research, or do homework for another class. Just sign and date the back of the coupon and return it to the teacher.

COUPON
LIBRARY PASS
Use this coupon to go to the library to read, research, or do homework for another class. Just sign and date the back of the coupon and return it to the teacher.

COUPON
LIBRARY PASS
Use this coupon to go to the library to read, research, or do homework for another class. Just sign and date the back of the coupon and return it to the teacher.

COUPON
LIBRARY PASS
Use this coupon to go to the library to read, research, or do homework for another class. Just sign and date the back of the coupon and return it to the teacher.

COUPON
LIBRARY PASS
Use this coupon to go to the library to read, research, or do homework for another class. Just sign and date the back of the coupon and return it to the teacher.

COUPON
LIBRARY PASS
Use this coupon to go to the library to read, research, or do homework for another class. Just sign and date the back of the coupon and return it to the teacher.

COUPON
LIBRARY PASS
Use this coupon to go to the library to read, research, or do homework for another class. Just sign and date the back of the coupon and return it to the teacher.

COUPON
LIBRARY PASS
Use this coupon to go to the library to read, research, or do homework for another class. Just sign and date the back of the coupon and return it to the teacher.

COUPON
Skip a Quiz/Homework
Use this coupon in place of a quiz on homework assignment. Just sign and date the back of the coupon and return it to the teacher at the time of redemption.

COUPON
Skip a Quiz/Homework
Use this coupon in place of a quiz on homework assignment. Just sign and date the back of the coupon and return it to the teacher at the time of redemption.

COUPON
Skip a Quiz/Homework
Use this coupon in place of a quiz on homework assignment. Just sign and date the back of the coupon and return it to the teacher at the time of redemption.

COUPON
Skip a Quiz/Homework
Use this coupon in place of a quiz on homework assignment. Just sign and date the back of the coupon and return it to the teacher at the time of redemption.

COUPON
Skip a Quiz/Homework
Use this coupon in place of a quiz on homework assignment. Just sign and date the back of the coupon and return it to the teacher at the time of redemption.

COUPON
Skip a Quiz/Homework
Use this coupon in place of a quiz on homework assignment. Just sign and date the back of the coupon and return it to the teacher at the time of redemption.

COUPON
Skip a Quiz/Homework
Use this coupon in place of a quiz on homework assignment. Just sign and date the back of the coupon and return it to the teacher at the time of redemption.

COUPON
Skip a Quiz/Homework
Use this coupon in place of a quiz on homework assignment. Just sign and date the back of the coupon and return it to the teacher at the time of redemption.

COUPON
One free
bathroom/water pass.
Use this coupon for a free trip to the bathroom or water fountain during class. Just sign the back of the coupon and return it to the teacher at the time of redemption.

COUPON
One free
bathroom/water pass.
Use this coupon for a free trip to the bathroom or water fountain during class. Just sign the back of the coupon and return it to the teacher at the time of redemption.

COUPON
One free
bathroom/water pass.
Use this coupon for a free trip to the bathroom or water fountain during class. Just sign the back of the coupon and return it to the teacher at the time of redemption.

COUPON
One free
bathroom/water pass.
Use this coupon for a free trip to the bathroom or water fountain during class. Just sign the back of the coupon and return it to the teacher at the time of redemption.

COUPON
One free
bathroom/water pass.
Use this coupon for a free trip to the bathroom or water fountain during class. Just sign the back of the coupon and return it to the teacher at the time of redemption.

COUPON
One free
bathroom/water pass.
Use this coupon for a free trip to the bathroom or water fountain during class. Just sign the back of the coupon and return it to the teacher at the time of redemption.

COUPON
One free
bathroom/water pass.
Use this coupon for a free trip to the bathroom or water fountain during class. Just sign the back of the coupon and return it to the teacher at the time of redemption.

COUPON
One free
bathroom/water pass.
Use this coupon for a free trip to the bathroom or water fountain during class. Just sign the back of the coupon and return it to the teacher at the time of redemption.

COUPON

One free test question equal to
no more than 5 points.

On a test, you are allowed to skip
one test question equal to no
more than 5 points. Just sign the
back of the coupon and staple it
to the test.

COUPON

One free test question equal to
no more than 5 points.

On a test, you are allowed to skip
one test question equal to no
more than 5 points. Just sign the
back of the coupon and staple it
to the test.

COUPON

One free test question equal to
no more than 5 points.

On a test, you are allowed to skip
one test question equal to no
more than 5 points. Just sign the
back of the coupon and staple it
to the test.

COUPON

One free test question equal to
no more than 5 points.

On a test, you are allowed to skip
one test question equal to no
more than 5 points. Just sign the
back of the coupon and staple it
to the test.

COUPON

One free test question equal to
no more than 5 points.

On a test, you are allowed to skip
one test question equal to no
more than 5 points. Just sign the
back of the coupon and staple it
to the test.

COUPON

One free test question equal to
no more than 5 points.

On a test, you are allowed to skip
one test question equal to no
more than 5 points. Just sign the
back of the coupon and staple it
to the test.

COUPON

One free test question equal to
no more than 5 points.

On a test, you are allowed to skip
one test question equal to no
more than 5 points. Just sign the
back of the coupon and staple it
to the test.

COUPON

One free test question equal to
no more than 5 points.

On a test, you are allowed to skip
one test question equal to no
more than 5 points. Just sign the
back of the coupon and staple it
to the test.

Social Reinforcers

PRAISE:

Good.
That's right.
Excellent.
That's interesting.
Thank you.
I'm pleased.
Exactly.
Good job.
Good thinking.
That's clever
I like that.
Great.
Good for you.
Not bad.
Super. Fantastic.
Fine. Marvelous.
Perfect.
Congratulations.
That was first class work!
You really pay attention!
That shows a great deal of work!
Now you have the hang of it.
You did a lot of work today.
That's quite an improvement.
I'm very proud of you today.
Nothing can stop you now.
You should show this to your father.
Show grandmom your picture.
You really out did yourself today.
I'm happy to see you working like that.
Boy, your brain is in high gear today!
You're working beautifully today.

EXPRESSIONS:

Smiling
Winking
Nodding
Laughing
Clapping
Blowing Kisses

CONTACT:

Touching
Hugging
Hold Hand
Sitting in Lap
Shaking Hand

CONTACT: (Cont.)

Patting head/shoulder
Walking together
Sitting together
Eating together
Playing games
Sharing
Touching elbows

ACTIVITY REINFORCERS:

Games
Trips
Messengers
Goody bags
Grab bags
Piñata
Answering telephone
Cleaning chalkboard
Listening to records
Extra playground time
Making bulletin board
Caring for AV equipment
Collecting cookie money
Looking for filmstrips
Helping custodian
Sitting with friends
Working in a special spot
Helping a friend
Free time
Knitting
Leading games
Crocheting
Taking attendance
Caring for plants
Caring for animals

TOKEN REINFORCERS:

Certificates
Points
Stars
Stamps
Happy Notes
Chips
Special Colors
Name Pins
Desk Signs
Buttons

Quick Tip
The Wrong Ways to
Express Disapproval

That's impractical.
Be prompt.
Work faster.
Try to understand.
Do your homework
Do your best
That's an unclear explanation.
Don't you want to do things right?
It can't be that difficult
You're too slow
stop talking
Behave.
Pay attention.
Don't.
Wrong.
Stupid.
Be still.
Follow directions.
Think for a change.
Use some thought.
No, that's not what I said.
Would you like to get paddled?
You don't understand because
      you don't listen.

That needs improving.
Mock me and you won't
      hear the end of it.
Shut up!
Don't be crabby.
That's ugly.
You're just boring.
Do it now.
You're not thinking
We'll never do this again.
You must be confused.
You'll wind up digging ditches.
You haven't applied yourself.

Maddening
Listen to me.
Stop.
Shh!
Absolutely not!
Horrible!
You're not doing as well.
Grow up!
Can't you spell?
I can't read your writing?
That's not mature.
Quit making messes.
What is this?
That's terrible.
Don't be silly.
I dislike that
What is that?
That's useless.
You should be ashamed.
You're gutless.
That's too vague.
Be quiet and sit down!
If I catch you chewing gum
      again, you'll wear it on
      your nose.

Be quiet.
Cut it out.
I'll give you something
      to cry about.
You have a dirty mind.
I'll show you who is boss.
Smart aleck.
Don't be a fraidycat.
Sit up straight.
Here's another "0".
I am the boss
Just try that again.

Chapter 7
Severe Discipline Problems

Focus

1. **To define at-risk students.**

2. **To identify strategies for disciplining severe behavior problems.**

3. **To analyze cultural differences and potential discipline problems.**

The good news is that most students want to behave appropriately in the classroom. The SWO students (Sit and Watch Others) make up about two-thirds of the classroom. These students are usually very good and are seldom if ever a discipline problem. They take their cues from other class members and react accordingly. Usually eye contact or close proximity with the teacher quickly bring them back to appropriate behavior. A second group, the PIL students (Push It a Little) require a more aggressive and assertive management plan. These students, who make up about thirty percent of the class, will carry inappropriate behavior further than the SWO students and will not stop immediately after the first warning. Eventually, however, they do respond to logical consequence and return to appropriate behaviors. The third group, MLS students (Mean Little Sugars), make up about five percent of the class. Their goal is to disrupt instruction, interfere with others, and make life miserable for teachers. Rules for these students have little if any meaning and consequences have no impact. These same students keep appearing on suspension, detention, tardy and absentee lists and show no remorse for their behavior; educators in their frustrated state continue to do the same things—the same things that are not working.

William Glasser, Richard Curwin, and Alan Mendler have made contributions to understanding students who are chronic misbehaviors.

Their main focus is empowering students with the responsibility for their own behaviors. These models will be discussed in greater detail later in this chapter.

At-Risk Students

The at-risk student in the regular classroom is a challenge to any teacher. The term "at-risk" refers to students who are unlikely to graduate from high school because of low achievement, financial obligations, lack of motivation, learning, disabilities, domestic demands, bilingualism, or severe discipline problems. Because American schools are designed to meet the needs of analytical, Caucasian middle-class students, teachers sometimes fail to meet the learning, behavioral, and communication styles of students from other ethnic or socioeconomic backgrounds. Over 80% of at-risk students are global (Marshall and Johns, 1992) and can not reach their full learning potential in the regular school environment. Because their personal needs for belonging, power, fun, and freedom are not met, these students resort to mistaken goals identified by Dreikurs only to meet failure, power struggles, and disapproval. When dealing with these populations, the principles of effective discipline include:

- the termination of "traditional" and ineffective discipline strategies.
- the redefinition of "fair" to mean that everyone will NOT always be treated the same.
- the development of rules through student participation.
- the development of meaningful consequences.
- the ownership of behavior by students.
- the empowerment of students to make responsible decisions about their behavior.

William Glasser and At-Risk Students

Prior to 1985, William Glasser's Reality Therapy had a great impact on public education. From his early theory, educators began using such buzz words as logical consequences, accept no excuses, classroom meetings, student choice, and self-control. Based on his theory, teachers were to establish meaningful classroom rules with logical consequences and accept no student excuses for "why" he/she misbehaved. All students were to be held accountable for their misbehavior and were to develop plans for alternative behaviors for similar situations in the future. Teachers had the responsibility of suggesting alternatives and reviewing student behavior plans or contracts. Some samples of these plans and contracts are found in Examples 7-A, 7-B, 7-C, and 7-D.

After 1985, Glasser dramatically changed his concept of classroom discipline and added terms such as "control theory," "quality schools," and "quality teachers." He no longer viewed schools as friendly, academic places but as boring places requiring students to complete repetitive, unmeaningful assignments as they sat and waited for the school day to end (1986). He no longer placed the sole responsibility for learning and behavior on students, but on schools and teachers responsible for providing a quality education. According to Glasser, school districts should redesign their curricula to meet student needs and should provide alternative assessment methods that encourage students to do their best work. Quality teachers serve as leaders rather than bosses and provide encouragement, stimulation, and an unending willingness to help students with academic and behavioral problems. Traditional classroom instruction should be replaced by meaningful content and student centered activities.

Example 7 - A
Student Plan

Student: _____ Date: _____

Teacher: _____

1. What is the problem?

2. How did I contribute to the situation?

3. Was this against the rules?

4. Did my actions help solve the problem?

5. What am I willing to do to solve the problem?

6. When will I start?

_____ _____ _____
        Student   Principal/ Counselor   Teacher

Follow up summary:

_____
        Teacher

Example 7 - B
Self-Control Plan

Name: _____ **Date:** _____

1. Behavior to be controlled:

2. Ideas that would help to control the behavior:

3. Things that will make it hard to control the behavior:

4. Plan for controlling the behavior:

5. Follow Up--Did the plan work? Why or why not/

6. The plan can be improved by:

Example 7 - C
Student Self-Analysis

Name: _____ Date: _____

Teacher: _____ Period: _____

The questions on this sheet will help you think about what happened and what can be done to prevent it from happening again. Please answer each question honestly.

1. What did I do that was inappropriate?

2. What did I want to happen?
___ I wanted to be in charge of the situation.
___ I wanted to challenge the teacher's authority.
___ I wanted to avoid doing work.
___ I wanted to be sent home.
___ I wanted to be noticed by the teacher and/or my peers.
___ I wanted to get even with someone.
___ Other_____

3. Did I get what I wanted?
Yes, because _____

No, because _____

4. Could I have gotten what I wanted in any other way?
Yes, I could have _____

No, because _____

5. What could I do so that this won't happen again?

6. My solution to this problem is

7. **This solution will help because**

8. **This solution will affect others because**

9. **The person who can help me achieve my goal is** _____.

10. **I will start my plan** _____

11. **If I fail to keep my contract, these are suitable consequences:**

This agreement has been formulated to help me maintain acceptable behavior in and out of the classroom.

_____   _____
             Student   **Teacher**

_____
           Date

Example 7 - D
Student Contract

Name: _____ Date: _____

Description of the problem:

Individuals involved with the intervention:
___ Student ___Parent
___ Teacher ___Administrator
___ Other ___ Counselor

Who will implement the plan?

How will the intervention be implemented?

Where will the intervention take place?

When will the intervention take place?

How will the person be reinforced?

What terminal behavior must be demonstrated before this intervention can be considered successful?

This is to verify that an agreement has been reached to implement the above intervention under the conditions specified.

_____   _____
      Signature   **Signature**

Considering the suggestions of Glasser and the realities of a school system held accountable by the public it serves, teachers may view Glasser's method as unrealistic. However, they may want to implement parts of his model by:

- providing interesting curriculum content.
- giving students choices in topics, learning methods, and assessment.
- conducting class meetings to resolve issues.
- supporting and praising students.
- offering assistance when students misbehave by discussing their inappropriate behavior and seeking solutions.

Disciplining students with Glasser's model becomes a very personal one-on-one conference in which the teacher will ask the student what he/she was doing, if that behavior will help him/her meet personal classroom goals, and what plan can be developed so that personal goals can be met. Its use will require time, patience, and energy on the part of the teacher but has proven successful with some at-risk students.

Curwin and Mendler--Discipline with Dignity

Richard Curwin and Allen Mendler recommend a variety of non-traditional methods in disciplining problem students. A key principle of their method is providing hope for students because without hope for success, students do not care if they fail, misbehave, or attend school. Teachers can assist students in regaining hope by providing interesting lessons on meaningful topics and guaranteeing degrees of success for all students. Another key principle is student dignity or respect for oneself and others. Students who daily experience failure naturally fight to preserve their dignity and usually use inappropriate behaviors to accomplish their goals. Teachers who view their role as confrontive when dealing with these students only add to the problem. Mendler describes the out of control student as one who has experienced failure, who has received most punishments and/or consequences offered at the school, who associates with similar type students, and who has been identified by various negative labels. Why then would any teacher want to try to reach this type of student? The truth of the matter is that many of these students are reachable by a few teachers and working with this type of student provides opportunities for teachers to improve their teaching skills and to enhance their supportive techniques.

A third principle is that traditional discipline methods do not work. Some students who chronically misbehave are immune to scolding, nagging, name-calling, threatening, detaining, and suspending. The following strategies are suggested in dealing with severe discipline problems.

- Relate subject content to the student personally
- Expose the student to a variety of good role models
- Speak informally with the student often
- Allow time for class meetings
- Assign projects that guarantee success
- Address individual learning styles
- Use I-messages
- "Catch 'em Being Good"
- Ignore some bad behavior
- Give a shot of attention
- Utilize one-on-one conferences with students to discuss problems
- Provide consistent academic help to students
- Remove any object or person creating a problem
- Satiate the student with the misbehavior. For example, a student who constantly talks in class serves detention where he/she must talk non-stop for the full detention time.
- Use humor in class

- Force parents to be involved

- Contract with students

- Use paradoxes. For example, a student who never does homework is complimented for being consistent.

- Share the bottom line with students by outlining their choices

- Use active listening

Finally, Curwin and Mendler stress the importance of student responsibility and the role of the teacher in allowing students to make choices, experience the results of their choices, and assist them in developing alternatives. Teachers are at schools to serve students, and part of every teacher's role is assisting students to develop responsible and meaningful lives. Disciplining a student with dignity requires time, non-traditional discipline strategies, and patience, but eventually, some of these difficult students rediscover hope and personal dignity and find their places in schools.

Activity 7-A
Classroom Situations

Instructions: Examine each of the situations below. How would Glasser address the issue? Curwin and Mendler?

1. How do you deal with children who continually exhibit inappropriate behavior such as talking, late papers, etc. Detention hall, parent/teacher conferences, etc. have been used but to no avail.

Glasser   Curwin/Mendler

2. How do you get rid of the classroom buzz? Rules have been set up and enforced, but the problem continues to exist.

Glasser   Curwin/ Mendler

3. How should parents be handled who complain about discipline practices that are unfair?

Glasser   Curwin/Mendler

4. What do you do when a student uses foul language in the classroom?

Glasser   Curwin/Mendler

5. When should students be sent to the office, and when should teachers handle their own behavior problems?

Glasser   Curwin/Mendler

6. How should students be handled who continually break dress code?

Glasser   Curwin/Mendler

7. Prior to any school holiday such as Christmas break, spring break, etc., the students who are considered to be severe discipline problems become even more of a problem. Why?

Glasser   Curwin/Mendler

8. How does a teacher successfully diffuse a group of students who are behaving inappropriately?

Glasser   Curwin/Mendler

9. How do you handle a student who adamantly refuses to do what you ask such as moving to another desk?

Glasser   Curwin/Mendler

10. What should a teacher do to prevent students from acting in a violent manner particularly when the parents tell these students that it is okay to hit someone else?

Glasser   Curwin/Mendler

Cultural Diversity and Discipline

Cultural differences sometimes create confusion, tension, and mistrust in a classroom. What seems logical, sensible, important and reasonable to a person in one culture may seem irrational, stupid, and unimportant to another. Due to a lack of cultural awareness, teachers and/or students misinterpret the motive for a behavior and a power struggle begins. In working with students from diverse cultures, teachers should know their own roots, prejudices, assumptions, and expectations; recognize that diversity occurs within groups; be tolerant, open, and flexible; observe and research more; know family members; promote cultural acceptance and equity; and listen to students and their families. The elements of a culture to be explored include:

- Ceremony
- Courtship and marriage
- Esthetics
- Ethics
- Health and medicine
- Family ties
- Gestures
- Grooming
- Personal behavior
- Ownership of property
- Rewards and Privileges
- Rights and Duties
- Religion
- Sex Roles
- Space and proxemics
- Subsistence
- Taboos
- Concepts of time
- Values

Example 7-E identifies several behaviors common to African-Americans, Native-Americans, Hispanic-Americans, and Asian-Americans.

Example 7 - E

Culturally Diverse Behaviors

African-Americans are likely to:

- Look away while listening

- Stand close to others while talking

- Be reluctant to share family problems and personal relationships

- Be concerned with present goals

- Consider family as very important

- Considers the mother's role as most significant in the family

- Believe that most within the white culture do not understand them

- Consider religion an important part of life and the minister as a community influence

- Consider elderly community members to be important and respected

- Live in a female headed household

Native-Americans are likely to:

- Demonstrate respect through "noninterference"

- Look away or down when interacting with adults

- Not challenge the opinion of an elder

- Work for the good of the group

- Share and expect reciprocity

- Be silent due to respect or uncertainty

- Be respectful of body space

- Do not distinguish between work and play since work is a place for humor and friendship

- Be relaxed about time

- Be very people-centered

- Observe and listen to learn a task

- Not engage in a task until they feel that they can succeed

Hispanic-Americans are likely to:

- Touch people when they speak to them
- Stand close to people when they speak
- Interpret prolonged eye contact as disrespectful
- Keep personal information confidential
- Have high regard for family
- Treat the elderly with respect
- Help other family members with child care
- Be nonconfrontational
- Be emotionally expressive Consider children a family priority
- Expect children to consult parents about important decisions
- Be more concerned with present rather than future time
- Be modest
- Have traditional male and female sex roles

Asian-Americans are likely to:

- Not shake hands
- Consider the touching of strangers as inappropriate
- Consider eye to eye contact as shameful
- Avoid conflict
- Consider emotional restraint, formality, and politeness as essential for appropriate social behavior
- Be nonconfrontational
- Be very modest
- Respect learning and have high educational standards
- Consider the behavior of a family member as a reflection on the entire family
- Consider family as important
- Hide emotional expressions
- Consider time as flexible

Activity 7 - B
Cultural Differences

Instructions: Examine the list of cultural behaviors on Example 7-E. Identify those that might be misinterpreted as inappropriate behavior for the classroom. How might the issue be resolved?

Behavior   **Misinterpretation**   **Resolution**

REFLECTION

1. How should you view chronic behavior problems in the classroom?

2. Do you think that schools must change to meet student needs or students must change to conform to school standards? Why?

3. What is your greatest fear about confronting a student who is behaving inappropriately?

4. List the steps you would take in helping a student improve his/her behavior.

Quick Tip
Learning Styles
Some Instructional Strategies for the Classroom

ENVIRONMENT:

1. Play music in the background during independent practice or group work. Be sure that it is something to which the students do not know the words.

2. Have a reading center for students to listen to recorded text materials.

3. A trip to a second hand store will yield fans, sweaters/jackets, old lamps, huge pillows, lawn chairs, and even a hammock. Use the fans and sweaters/jackets to provide appropriate temperature or use seating assignments near windows or doors to meet special needs. Lamps can be used to brighten certain corners or soften lighting in the room. During certain periods of the class, allow students to go to designated areas for informal seating or arrange the classroom in a "U" shape rather than traditional rows.

4. Allow students to sit on the floor for some activities such as watching a VCR tape.

EMOTIONAL:

1. Break assignments down into smaller parts.

2. Praise students often for their successes.

3. Address the student's need for freedom by allowing him/her choices in assignments and in grading criteria.

4. Use portfolios in assessment.

5. Provide detailed assignment sheets for analytical students. Within a lesson, model for students and allow for guided practice.
When giving directions, questions students as to what they are to do.

6. Give several long term assignments utilizing calendars for analytical students.

SOCIOLOGICAL:

1. Provide for choices if students wish to work alone or in groups.

2. Provide for organized group work that challenges higher order thinking.

3. Allow students to write notes to each other when they have completed assignments or have mailbox slots for students to put "mail" for classmates.

4. Assign peer tutors for students. When a student has a question, he/she can ask the peer tutor first before going to the teacher.

5. Develop study groups for meeting outside of class.

PHYSICAL:

1. When lecturing, always use a visual. An outline of the lecture serves as an organizer as well as paces the lesson.

2. Use as many manipulatives as possible.

3. Bring in outside materials.

4. Take students on field trips

5. Allow a student to be a "runner" in a group activity

6. Act out periods or stories; Video tape students when possible.

7. Have classes outdoors or in other locations besides the classroom.

8. Provide popcorn, mints, and/or gum for students who need intake. Have water and paper cups in the room for students who need to drink. Eating/drinking should be considered a privilege for students. Any abuse of the privilege will end it.

9. Use colors to highlight information.

10. Allow rest time for students.

11. Have students use notebooks with a "wide rule" and develop "doodle" columns.

INSTRUCTION:

1. When assigning several pages to be read, have students write a multiple choice type question on an index card for every 2-3 pages read. These cards become good sources for game competitions and student review. Some of the questions can be used on the test.

2. When reading assignments, select shared reading in which the teacher reads a segment of the assignment and then uses convergent and divergent questions to check for comprehension. Then, the teacher calls on a student to read an unspecified segment. Once again, the teacher or student will ask questions to check comprehension, and another student will be named to read. If at some point the questions can not be answered, students are instructed to use their index fingers to follow along in the text. The question is then repeated. Students are called on at random to read and to respond to questions.

3. Rather than read from a textbook, use the newspaper or current high-interest magazines for instructional purposes. This strategy can be used in English, social studies, and science classes.

4. Collect samples of student writing and with their permission allow the other students to read the paragraphs, essays, and short stories in class. Develop lessons around these sample selections.

5. Have students read a story in class, but stop before the climax. Have students write the ending.

6. Recall a story that students have read or know from childhood such as Cinderella or Mother Goose rhymes. Have students tell the story from another point of view.

7. Record stories on audio tape to be used at a learning center in the classroom. Students could do this as part of an assignment.

8. Develop plays and/or skits from reading text.

9. Select 2 to 3 fiction stories and have students combine characters, settings, etc. to create new stories.

10. Use choral readings or have students create poems from prose writings.

11. Develop flashcards for vocabulary words. Use a 5X7 card and divide it into 4 areas. In one area, the student writes the word; in a second area, the student draws a picture of the word's meaning; in space three, students define the word; in space 4, the students write an antonym for the word.

12. Roulette writing Have all students write for two minutes on a defined topic such as a reading assignment or fiction topic. At the end of two minutes, all students pass their papers back, read their new paper, and write for two minutes more. This process continues until each student has his/her original paper back.

13. Use highlighters to help students organize information. This can also be used with folders, notebook paper, etc.

14. Train students to use memory aids such as acronyms (HOMES-Huron, Ontario, Michigan, Erie, and Superior) or chaining sentences (Aunt Alice ate apples nearly every Saturday - Africa, Asia, Australia, Antarctica, North America, Europe, and South America).

15. Visualization is helpful. For example, if a student is trying to remember steps to a problem, have him/her picture his/her house. As he/she walks through each room, mentally have him/her relate the order of the movement through rooms to the steps in solving the problem.

16. Use a whole language approach when teaching. For example, combine units with social studies, computer literacy, science, and English.

17. Allow students to brainstorm ideas and assist in grouping these.

18. Post information around the classroom such as vocabulary, math formulas, etc.

19. Have students to use tape recorders and orally write. Later these can be transcribed and corrected.

20. Use computers and calculators in class.

21. Allow students to go to the blackboard, paper easel, or use individual slates.

22. Utilize a variety of games that allow the players to spin or throw dice and move around a gameboard.

23. Use lesson outlines.

24. Give students pre-reading questions.

25. Clearly post, state, and have students copy daily objectives.

Quick Tip
Problem Solving Sequence for
Behavioral Consultation

1. **Define and clarify the problem.**
   What is the problem?
   What is contributing to the problem?
   What other alternatives have been tried in the past?

2. **Analyze the forces contributing to the problem.**
   What factors contribute to the problem?
   What events consistently precede the problem behavior?
   What events consistently follow the problem behavior?
   What are the behavior expectations of the student by the teacher and parents?
   What specific outcomes do the teacher and parents have?
   How willing are the teacher and parents to do certain interventions to help the student?

3. **Discuss alternative solutions.**

4. **Evaluate and choose the best alternative.**
   Will the choice decrease the inappropriate behavior?
   What consequences will be used?

5. **Specify the responsibilities of the party members.**

6. **Implement the plan.**

7. **Evaluate the plan for effectiveness.**
   Is the plan working?
   If not, what other alternative should be tried?

Quick Tip
Power Struggles

1. Power struggles are "no win" situations.

2. Active listening allows the teacher to listen without agreeing or disagreeing with the student. The teacher merely acknowledges what the student says by facial gestures and paraphrasing.

3. Allow for "cool down" time. When two parties are angry, nothing can be accomplished. Set up a time to speak later.

4. All communication should be confidential. Never try to settle a confrontation in front of the student's peers.

5. Never embarrass the student.

6. Once cleared with the principal, implement the insubordination rule with any student who refuses to accept a consequence. Until the student is ready to cooperate, he/she will not be allowed back in the classroom.

Quick Tip
Steps to Reality Therapy

1. Involvement - Students must be involved in changing their own behavior.

2. Focusing on present behavior - The focus is on the current behavior and feelings are not emphasized.

3. Evaluating behavior - Students are asked if their behavior is appropriate or inappropriate.

4. Planning responsible behavior - The student develops a plan to alter his/her behavior.

5. Commitment - Students are required to commit to the plan.

6. Responsibility - It is the responsibility of the student to improve his/her behavior. "Why" a plan fails is not a concern of the teacher. The focus remains on the inappropriate behavior and what can be done to modify that behavior. The teacher must make it clear to students that excuses are unacceptable.

7. Eliminate punishment and use logical consequences.

Quick Tip
PEP Method

When students break a rule, utilize proximity, eye contact, and privacy (PEP) to handle the situation.

1. Move into the student's space (Proximity).

2. Make direct eye-contact with the student when delivering the message (Eye Contact).

3. Make certain that the only person who hears the message is the student to whom it is directed (Privacy).

Quick Tip
Student Fights

Why do students fight?
1. To save face
2. To defend property
3. To compensate for fear
4. To test the pecking order

How do I stop a fight?
1. Send for help.
2. Remove the audience
3. Approach the fighting students and make a loud noise by clapping your hands or shouting.
4. Identify the more aggressive student.
5. When help arrives, separate the students.

Quick Tip
Characteristics of ADD/ADHD Students

Students with attention deficit disorder and attention deficit hyperactivity disorder demonstrate the following characteristics:

Fidgets, squirms, and is restless
Can not remain seated
Is easily distracted
Has difficulty waiting for his/her turn
Blurts out answers
Has difficulty following instructions
Has difficulty sustaining attention
Shifts from one uncompleted task to another
Can not play quietly
Talks excessively
Interrupts others
Does not seem to listen
Often loses things
Engages in dangerous activities
Procrastinates

Some classroom accommodations/modifications for these students might include:
1. Shorten the work session
2. Select activities that are short term or break down large tasks into smaller components.
3. Allow students to take a break
4. Seat the student in the front of the room away from doors and windows.
5. Tape a list of daily activities on the student's desk.
6. Require students to keep personal item away from his/her desk.
7. Require that pencils/pens be down during instruction time.
8. Require students to use folded columns or paper covers to direct attention to one item or problem.
9. Have students delay answering questions until they have time to think.
10. Avoid busy rooms.
11. Prepare cubicles for individual work.
12. Display materials away from the students.
13. Allow students extra time.
14. Have students keep desks clear.
15. Post rules in the classroom.
16. Monitor progress often using proximity and eye contact.
17. Eliminate or reduce the number of timed tests.
18. Develop schedules to prevent procrastination.
19. Communicate with parents through written notebooks, forms, etc.
20. Provide daily structure and routines.

Quick Tip
Student Opinion of Teaching

Below are several statements written about your teacher. Read each statement carefully, and then circle the number which indicates how you feel about the statement with 5 meaning you strongly agree and 1 meaning you strongly disagree.

5 4 3 2 1   1. Activities are related to my interests and needs.

5 4 3 2 1   2. The classroom is organized.

5 4 3 2 1   3. I receive encouragement and support in class.

5 4 3 2 1   4. I understand the learning objectives my teacher has for me.

5 4 3 2 1   5. Classwork is challenging.

5 4 3 2 1   6. I have the opportunity to participate in planning activities.

5 4 3 2 1   7. The class has a variety of activities.

5 4 3 2 1   8. The teacher is courteous and respectful to students.

5 4 3 2 1   9. The teacher informs me of my progress over a grading period.

5 4 3 2 1   10. The tests are representative of the material covered in class.

Below is a list of adjectives. Check each word that describes your teacher.

___ supportive   ___intelligent   ___friendly
___ fair   ___prepared   ___enthusiastic
___ flexible   ___humorous   ___thorough
___ creative   ___fun   ___understanding

Comments:

Quick Tip
Teacher Assessment

Please help me improve my teaching by completing this form. DO NOT PUT YOUR NAME ON THIS SHEET.

1. Rate your teacher from 1 - 10 on the following items with 10 being the highest.
___ Neatness   ___ Helpfulness   ___Enthusiasm
___ Preparedness   ___ Caring   ___ Availability
___ Discipline   ___ Fairness   ___Creativity

2. What did you like best about this class?

3. What did you like least?

4. If you could change one thing about this class, what would you change?

5. Give your teacher a letter grade (A, B, C, D, or F) for the school year.

Teacher Assessment

Please help me improve my teaching by completing this form. DO NOT PUT YOUR NAME ON THIS SHEET.

1. Rate your teacher from 1 - 10 on the following items with 10 being the highest.
___ Neatness   ___ Helpfulness   ___Enthusiasm
___ Preparedness   ___ Caring   ___ Availability
___ Discipline   ___ Fairness   ___Creativity

2. What did you like best about this class?

3. What did you like least?

4. If you could change one thing about this class, what would you change?

5. Give your teacher a letter grade (A, B, C, D, or F) for the school year.

Chapter 8
Parent/Teacher Partnerships

```
┌─────────────────────────────────────────────────────────────┐
│                          Focus                                │
│                                                               │
│  1.  To develop successful parent/teacher partnerships.       │
│  2.  To conduct productive parent/teacher conferences.        │
└─────────────────────────────────────────────────────────────┘
```

How to deal with parents is one of those gray areas for which new teachers receive minimal training. Yet, it is an important component when dealing with children. When asked, parents describe an effective teacher as one who can discipline students and who desires to work with parents. However, nothing is more frightening to a new or seasoned teacher than an irate parent defending his/her child. There are certain things that teachers can do to promote positive communication and cooperation from parents.

I. Establish and communicate classroom standards

Parents should be informed of classroom policies and procedures at the beginning of the school year. This can be achieved through letters to parents, phone calls, and conferences. At the beginning of the school year, parents should be notified in writing of classroom rules, homework policies, grading procedures, and routines such as make-up work. In the correspondence, the teacher should encourage parent participation through volunteer services and should include a schedule of available times for conferences. There should be a place for the parent to sign the document, and the teacher should keep on file the returned signature. If after a reasonable time the parent has not returned the signed portion of the document, a call should be made to inquire about the delay.

II. Establish positive communication with parents

Some parents only hear from the school when a child is in trouble. Teachers should make a point of "good news" calls and/or notes to inform parents of a child's success. Make it a habit to send home at least 5 positive notes each week and make at least 4 phone calls to parents. Certainly this can be time consuming, but not nearly as time consuming as dealing with an upset parent. Parents need to feel that teachers have a positive attitude toward students.

III. Document, document, document!

Develop a method for documenting problems in student behavior and academics. Included within the documentation should be times parents were contacted regarding the behavior/and or achievement of students. AN "F" ON A TEST OR ASSIGNMENT SHOULD BE AN AUTOMATIC CALL HOME; AN "A" ON A TEST OR AN ASSIGNMENT IS AN AUTOMATIC CALL HOME; A DRASTIC GRADE CHANGE EITHER POSITIVE OR NEGATIVE SHOULD BE AN AUTOMATIC CALL HOME; CHANGES IN BEHAVIOR, GOOD OR BAD, SHOULD BE ADDRESSED IMMEDIATELY THROUGH A PARENT NOTIFICATION. Keep all graded student work on file and document all contacts with parents.

IV. Ask for help at the first sign of a problem

Never allow a problem to snowball. Contact parents immediately when there is a change in grade or behavior. Parents can sometimes assist in explaining or clarifying reasons for the change.

V. Assertively seek the help of parents

What about parents who refuse to return calls or refuse to attend conferences? Remember that as a teacher, you have a right to parental support, and that only through cooperative efforts can you do your job effectively. Plan your conversation in advance, and use these notes to prevent sidetracking by parents. Always begin with a positive note about the student, state the problem specifically, offer suggestions when asked, end the conversation with a summary of responsibilities and expectations, and offer a positive comment such as "Thank you for being so helpful." ALWAYS FOLLOW UP CONVERSATIONS WITHIN A REASONABLE TIME. As the teacher, you should never apologize for contacting parents, never minimize the problem, or belittle your own abilities.

Conducting the Conference

When conducting a parent/teacher conference, follow these guidelines:

1. BE PREPARED! Prepare notes for the conference. Arrive on time. Have the room and halls well lit to welcome the parent(s).

2. Stand up to greet the parent and hold your discussion at a conferencing area with appropriate size table and chairs. Show interest in the parent, but avoid too much small talk.

3. Make eye contact with the parent and address him/her by name.

4. Mention positive traits of the student, and never surprise the parent(s) with a new problem.

5. After discussing the purpose of the conference, have student work available for the parent(s) to view or any documentation of the problem. Above all else, LISTEN.

6. Summarize the conference at the end.

7. Establish a follow-up date.

8. Have parent(s) sign the conference form.

9. File the notes from the conference

10. Follow up.

Remember that good parental relationships are on-going. As the teacher you have a right to parental support.

Example 8 - A

Use this checklist when preparing for a parent/teacher conference.

___ 1. Will there be privacy, free of noise and distractions?

___ 2. Is the conference site designed for adults to meet with adult sized chairs and a table?

___ 3. Are student records available?

___ 4. Have you completed the heading for a conference form with objectives clearly stated?

___ 5. Do you have a signed copy of the discipline plan letter?

___ 6. Is student work available to show parents?

Example 8-B
Parent Teacher Conference Form

Subject/Grade:_____ Date: _____ Time: _____

Student: _____ Teacher: _____

Type of Conference:
____ **Regularly scheduled school conference**
____ **Requested school conference**
____ **Telephone**
____ **Home/office visit**

Goals for the conference:

Objectives for the conference:

Assertions made to parents:

Information shared with parents:

Plan for improvement
    Parent's responsibility:

    Teacher's responsibility:

Follow up conference date:

Example 8 - C

School/Parent Telephone Record

Student: _____

Teacher: _____ Grade/Subject: _____

Parents/Guardian: _____

Phone Number(s): _____(work) _____(home)

Date	Time	Response #*	Purpose	Comments
1.				
2.				
3.				
4.				
5.				
6.				
7.				
8.				
9.				

*Response List:
1. Spoke with parent
2. Busy signal
3. No answer
4. Disconnected telephone
5. Scheduled call back _____
6. No adult home
7. Declined to speak
8. Family initiated call
9. Other _____

Comments:
_____
_____

Example 8 - D
Weekly Progress R· port
___ 6 Weeks

Date	Behavior M T W Th F	Assignments M T W Th F	Tests M T W Th F	Parent's Initials

Comments:

Weekly Progress Report
___ 6 Weeks

Date	Behavior M T W Th F	Assignments M T W Th F	Tests M T W Th F	Parent's Initials

Comments:

Example 8 - E
Student Progress

Name: _____Date: _____

Effort	Work Habits	Behavior
___ Outstanding	___ Works Independently	___ Is a Leader
___ Very Good	___ Needs Some Guidance	___ Sets a Good Example
___ Good	to Complete Work	___ Is Improving
___ Needs Improvement	___ Needs Constant	___ Forgets Self-Control
	Guidance to Complete	
	Assignments	
	___ Easily Distracted	
	___ Distracts Others	

___ If checked here, student is in need of the following supplies:

Test Scores:

_____   _____

_____   _____
      Teacher's Signature   Parent's Signature

Student Progress

Name: _____Date: _____

Effort	Work Habits	Behavior
___ Outstanding	___ Works Independently	___ Is a Leader
___ Very Good	___ Needs Some Guidance	___ Sets a Good Example
___ Good	to Complete Work	___ Is Improving
___ Needs Improvement	___ Needs Constant	___ Forgets Self-Control
	Guidance to Complete	
	Assignments	
	___ Easily Distracted	
	___ Distracts Others	

___ If checked here, student is in need of the following supplies:

Test Scores:

_____   _____

_____   _____
      Teacher's Signature   Parent's Signature

Example 8 - F
Weekly Assessment Sheet

Name:_____Dates_____

Teacher: _____

Below is a weekly report of your child's progress. Please read it carefully and initial it at the bottom. Please return it to school for your child's folder.

Scores: Tests: Homework:

Type	Score		Type	Score
_____	___		_____	___
_____	___		_____	___
_____	___		_____	___

The following observations were made:

___ Great week!
___ Incomplete assignments
___ Not following directions
___ Talking too much
___ Behavior needs improving

                    ****

___ Please call for a conference.

COMMENTS:

Parent's Initials: _____

Example 8 - F
Weekly Assessment Sheet

Name:_____Dates_____

Teacher: _____

Below is a weekly report of your child's progress. Please read it carefully and initial it at the bottom. Please return it to school for your child's folder.

Scores: Tests: Homework:

Type	Score		Type	Score
_____	___		_____	___
_____	___		_____	___
_____	___		_____	___

The following observations were made:

___ Great week!
___ Incomplete assignments
___ Not following directions
___ Talking too much
___ Behavior needs improving

                    ****

___ Please call for a conference.

COMMENTS:

Parent's Initials: _____

Example 8 - G
Student Self-Assessment

Name: _____

Week of: _____

Check the statement that best describes your week.

____ I had a great week! I did my best on most of my work and behaved well in class. The teacher is very pleased with me.

____ I had a good week as far as behavior goes, but I need to work more on my classroom assignments.

____ I had a good week as far as academics go, but I need to work on my behavior.

____ I had a fair week. My teacher and I agree that I could do better in my behavior and my school work.

Areas for Improvement

Please check those areas that you feel need improvement.

____ I need to study more for my tests next week.

____ I need to listen and follow directions on tests and classroom work.

____ I need to complete all of my classroom assignments.

____ I need to stop daydreaming in class.

____ I need to check my work before I turn in papers.

____ I need to do my homework every night.

____ I need to bring my books and supplies to class.

____ I need to stop talking in class so that I can hear instructions and do not disturb others.

____ I need to stay in my desk.

____ I need to get serious about my classwork and stop wasting time.

____ I need to return graded papers promptly.

____ I need to review all classroom routines and rules and follow them closely.

Important Dates to Remember

Date	Assignment/Activity Due
____	_____
____	_____
____	_____

Teacher Comments: _____

Parent Comments: _____

_____

Parent's Signature: _____

Chapter 9
A Final Activity

Now that you have completed this workbook, you should have put some

thought and planning into your first day as a teacher. Remember, classroom

management is more than a set of rules with consequences, and nothing takes the

place of a well planned lesson that involves students in activities that meet their

needs. The following activity will help you develop a comprehensive management

plan for your classroom.

Section I - INTRODUCTION

Section I is an overview of your personal discipline plan. For what grade
level and/or subject area is it intended? What do you know about the wants and
needs of students at this level? What are your special needs in the classroom? How
will this impact your management plan.

Section II - THE MODEL

This is the meat of your plan. Consider the following: 1. Classroom
procedures - What is the purpose of classroom procedures? How will you teach
these routines to students? Identify a minimum of 5 classroom procedures and how
they will benefit your classroom management. 2. Appropriate and inappropriate
behavior - how will you define them? What theoretical model(s) will you use?
What are your classroom rules? How did you develop these rules? Which mistaken
student goals do they meet? How will you convey these rules to students and
parents? 3. Consequences - What are the consequences for students breaking the
rules? How will these consequences be enforced? Remember that using academic material
for punish work is not acceptable, and the office is the last resort. 4. Individual and
group motivation - What will happen when a student does something right? What
forms of acknowledgment will be used? How will you motivate and reward the
entire group? How will you meet the individual needs of the students in you
classroom? 5. Preventive and supportive discipline - What techniques will you use
to prevent discipline problems? Why? 6. Physical arrangement - complete a diagram
of your classroom. Why have you chosen this type of classroom arrangement? How
do you expect this arrangement to impact the interaction in your classroom? If you
anticipate that your room arrangement may create problems, explain them and how
you will deal with them. How will your room arrangement solve discipline
problems? 7. Parental Involvement - How will parents be involved in the
management plan? How will they receive feedback.

Section III: MODEL APPLICATION

Explain a typical classroom situation--hypothetical or real--from start to finish. How would you deal with the situation based on your classroom management model? Describe the inappropriate behavior and your response to it. Does your plan work?

Classroom Management Plan Worksheet

Section I: Introduction

Section II: The Model

REFERENCES

Canter, L. & Hausner, L. (1987). <u>Homework without tears</u>. New York: Harper and Row.

Canter, L. & Canter, M. (1976). <u>Assertive discipline: A take-charge approach for today's educator</u>. Santa Monica, CA: Lee Canter & Associates.

Charles, C. M. (1996) <u>Building classroom discipline</u> (5th ed.). New York: Longman.

Curwin, R. L. & Mendler, A. N. (1988). <u>Discipline with dignity</u>. Alexandria, VA: ASCD.

Dreikurs, R., Grunwald, B. B., & Pepper, F. C. (1982). <u>Maintaining sanity</u> in the <u>classroom</u>. (2nd ed.) New York: Harper & Row.

Froyen, L. A. (1988). <u>Classroom management: Empowering teacher-leaders</u>. Columbus, OH: Merrill.

Ginott, H. G. (1972). <u>Teacher and child</u>. New York: Avon Books.

Glasser, W. (1986). <u>Control theory in the classroom</u>. New York: Harper and Row.

Glasser, W. (1975). <u>Schools without failure</u>. New York: Harper and Row.

Glasser, W. (1992). <u>The quality school: Managing students without coercion</u>. New York: Harper & Row.

Glasser, W. (1993). <u>The quality school teacher</u>. New York: Harper and Row.

Gray, J. (1974). <u>The teacher's survival guide</u>. Belmont: Fearon.

Grossman, H. (1990). <u>Trouble-free teaching: Solutions to behavior problems in the classroom</u>. Mountain View, CA: Mayfield.

Jocobsen, D., Eggen, P., & Kauchak, D. (1993). <u>Methods for teaching: A skills approach</u> (4th ed.). New York: Macmillan.

Kohut, S. & Range, D. G. (1992). <u>Classroom discipline: Case studies and viewpoints</u> (2nd ed.). Washington D. C.: National Education Association.

Lemleck, J. K. (1988). Classroom management: Methods and techniques for elementary and secondary teachers (2nd ed.). New York: Longman.

Long, J. D., Frye, V. H., & Long, E. W. (1989). Making it till Friday (4th ed.). Princeton: Princeton Book Company.

Macht, J. (1990). Managing classroom behavior: An ecological approach to academic and social learning. New York: Longman.

Marshall, C. & Johns, K. (1992). Success strategies for at-risk students. Dallas: Center for Success in Learning.

Marzano, R. J. (1992). A different kind of classroom: Teaching with dimensions of learning. Alexandria, VA: ASCD.

McCarthy, B., Leflar, S., & McNamara, M. M. The 4MAT workbook. Barrington: Excel, Inc.

Mendler, A. N. (1992). What do I do when. . . How to achieve discipline with dignity in the classsroom. Bloomington: National Education Service.

Rivers, L. W. (1986). The disruptive student and the teacher. Washington, D. C.: National Education Association.

Schell, L. M. & Burden, (1994). Countdown to the first day of school. West Haven: NEA Checklist Series.

Shuman, R. B. (1992). Classroom encounters: Problems, case studies, solutions. Washington, D. C.: National Education Association.

Swick, K. J. (1985). Maintaining productive student behavior. Washington D. C., National Education Association.

Swick, K. J. (1985). Parents and teachers as discipline shapers. Washington, D. C.: National Education Association.

Tauber, R. T. (1995). Classroom management: Theory and practice. Fort Worth: Harcourt Brace College Publishers.

Wong, H. K. & Wong, R. T. (1991). The first days of school. Sunnyvale: Harry K. Wong Publications.